Breeding Insects
as feeder food

David Haggett

Published by

Mantispress

www.mantispress.co.uk

Mantis Press
Peacehaven
East Sussex
United Kingdom
Visit us at *www.mantispress.co.uk*

First published in 2013
Second Edition December 2016
Copyright © in published edition, 2016: Mantis Press
Copyright © in text, 2016: David Haggett
Copyright © in photographs, 2016: David Haggett with the
following exception:
Green Banana roaches on page 32 – Virginia Cheeseman.

Editor: Lesley Haggett
Designer: Mantis Press

Printed by CreateSpace

Table of Contents

Introduction

Having been fortunate enough to live in Europe, Asia and South Africa, I have had the opportunity to breed a wide range of insects in different environments and diverse circumstances, over several decades.

Many of these insects were bred as part of a lifelong interest in entomology. When an opportunity arose to breed chameleons commercially, I also needed to generate large numbers of insects as food. Then the fun began!

There are many differences between rearing a few moth larvae as a hobby and the management of thousands of cockroaches or crickets. Different climates, finding suitable cages, obtaining breeding stock, problems with cold/heat/ants/landlords – have all made breeding insects in volume an interesting challenge. But also a rewarding one.

This is not an in-depth study of each insect group nor a coffee table book crammed with photographs. It is a guide on how to get started and successfully breed insects as food for insectivores. Each chapter follows a similar layout to make comparisons between species easier.

There are undoubtedly other methods that work well. I do not claim that what follows is the only way to succeed but, in every case, the method shown has worked well for me.

Although chameleons and mantis are mentioned frequently throughout, the advice is relevant to any insectivorous reptile, bird, mammal, arachnid or even insect.

Panther chameleon about to eat a mantis

Young Veiled chameleon aiming for a silkworm

Why breed your own insects?

In the past few decades there has been a phenomenal growth in the successful keeping of many hitherto 'difficult' species of captive animal, such as chameleons.

It is not just reptile keepers that need access to a constant supply of live insects. Praying mantis have also become very popular and the hobby is growing at a fast pace. Spiders, scorpions, assassin bugs and many other types of invertebrate are increasingly available and need live food.

There are many reasons for the current advances in the husbandry of reptiles, mantis and other insectivores. Our understanding of their needs has been matched by an increase in the availability of technology and equipment unheard of a few years ago, and at prices within the reach of the hobbyist. The range of species in captivity is greater than ever before and the ease with which so many species can be obtained is amazing.

In the wild, insectivores - reptile, mammal, bird and invertebrate - will have access to a wide range of types and species of insect. Yet in captivity they are frequently fed a monotonous diet. This is often the result of a limited selection of food types available at the local pet shop, seasonal restrictions or the expense involved in buying a variety of insects as foods.

Having gone to the trouble of setting up a vivarium to mirror its occupant's natural habitat, it seems a shame to risk the long-term well-being of the inhabitant by feeding it a limited and, possibly, unnatural diet.

The solution to that problem is the subject of this book – how to breed a wide range of feeder insects. Doing so will free you from the issues of availability, seasonality and some of the cost of providing a healthy variety of food for your animal.

One word of warning - if you follow the advice given you may find yourself getting absorbed by a fascinating new hobby – breeding insects for their own sake!

Wild-caught Insects?

If you catch insects in the wild be careful that they have not been subjected to insecticides. Some insects are naturally poisonous but these can normally be recognised by their colouring.

Panther chameleon eating a locust

Typically, the poisonous insects will include the brighter-coloured butterflies and flying insects. Red and orange colouration is a common sign to predators that an insect is unpalatable but the warnings colours vary by Continent. A captive-bred chameleon from Madagascar may not recognise a toxic insect from the United States and vice versa. It is wise to check in a good reference book before using an unfamiliar insect as food.

On the other hand, it would appear that many of the poisons that affect vertebrates are ineffectual on invertebrates. I have fed 'poisonous' butterflies to mantis with no ill-effects.

It is sensible to avoid any stinging or biting insect and those with spines; caterpillars with hairs or spines should also be avoided.

Feeder Insects

Basics

When considering what type of insect might be bred as food, the key requirements are that it breeds easily and produces a lot of off-spring. Unfortunately, the majority of insects that fall into that category are classified as pests.

Crickets, cockroaches, fruit flies, houseflies, etc., are easy to breed but can pose potential risks to a household. It is essential, therefore, that any container being used is escape-proof and that the method of feeding insects to your insectivore minimises the risks of escapees. It is very annoying to hear the constant screech of crickets at night, knowing that they are in your house because they escaped from your breeding colony. It might be difficult to get rid of an infestation of crickets or cockroaches.

Fortunately, most of the insects discussed in this book will die if subjected to cold temperatures.

Cages and heating

I mainly use plastic food or storage containers that are relatively cheap and easily obtained. There is such a variety of shapes and sizes available that you can use your imagination (and common sense) to adapt them to suit your purposes.

In many countries these plastic containers are sold in standard sizes, e.g. 25 litre or 80 litre. Since this is not the case in every country, I have added the approximate size in metric and converted to imperial, rounded to the nearest half inch. Rather than repeat the measurements throughout the book, these are the ones most commonly used:

- 5 litre container = 34cm x 20cm x 12.5cm high (13.5" x 8" x 5" high)
- 25 litre container = 42cm x 25cm x 32cm high (16.5" x 10" x 12.5" high)
- 80 litre container = 60cm x 40cm x 42cm high (24" x 16" x 16.5" high)

With a sharp knife and a hot-glue gun ventilation holes can be added, along with entry points for live food, hinged doors, etc. There are also many types of heating devices available today, with thermostats and timers.

As with any hobby that involves the use of knives and electricity, care is needed. Ensure that you follow any legal requirements and common sense.

Food

For the most part, the insects in this book are either omnivores or herbivorous. For these, reference is made to two types of food: 'wet' and dry.

Dry foods typically consist of fish flakes, dry dog or cat pellets, cereals such as oats, bran, etc.

'Wet' foods are fruit and vegetables. Despite their nickname, choose fruit and vegetables that do not have a high water content or that wilt quickly, for example: water melon and lettuce. Good 'wet' foods are carrots, apple, cabbage, squash, pumpkin and potatoes. Acid citrus fruits like lemons are best avoided.

All fruit and vegetables should be washed and free of pesticides. They should be dry when placed in the container. 'Wet' food can increase the humidity inside the container and should be monitored carefully to avoid a problem with mould. Any foods that show a sign of mould should be removed immediately (after checking that no small insects are hiding in holes in the food).

Gut Loading

The term 'gut loading' is sometimes misused or misunderstood. In some literature it refers to feeding the insects a special selection of nutritionally rich food in the 24 hour period prior to offering them to the insectivore.

In captivity, feeder insects are restricted in their diets to what you feed them. So the nutritional value of your feeder insect is only as good as the food it gets. If its regular diet is poor, then the cricket will be nutritionally poor and possibly unhealthy. For it to be as nutritionally valuable and as healthy as possible, it will need to have been fed good quality food throughout its life.

Providing better nutrition to the insect in the 24 hours before it is used as food may make some difference to the contents of its gut but normally no appreciable difference to its overall quality as a food item.

There are some who feel that 'gut loading', with a diet high in calcium, prior to feeding to a reptile can be useful. In most cases, you can achieve the same results by dusting the insect with calcium and vitamin powder when you feed it to your predator.

How much value can be added to an already healthy and well-fed cricket by 'gut loading' is open to debate. There will be some who insist that the 24 hour 'gut loading' ritual is important, while there are others who maintain that it is unnecessary if you are breeding your own feeder insects using a good diet.

The benefits of 'gut loading' commercially produced feeder insects are quite different. In such cases, you do not know what they have been fed previously, so anything that might increase the insects' nutritional value is probably positive.

Food items often suggested for 'gut loading' are:

Tropical fish flakes, squash or pumpkin, potatoes and sweet potatoes, carrots, oranges, apples, wheat germ, dry dog or cat food, leafy greens such as cabbage, mustard greens, kale, celery, etc.

You will note that these are similar to the food you would be feeding your feeder insects normally.

No matter what species you keep, cleanliness is important to prevent smell and disease. Turkestan roaches, *Shelfordella lateralis*, like all roaches, need regular cleaning as they produce a lot of waste and have their own unique odour!

Hygiene

When breeding any insect, cleanliness is imperative. This may seem a strange consideration given that many of them are pests. However,

Maggots can be smelly… and carry disease.

due to the large numbers being kept in close proximity, a lack of hygiene will quickly be noticed by a sudden rise in mortality and a noticeable increase in bad smells.

For the most part, breeding insects requires a mix of common sense and providing the right conditions. Insects, especially pests, are programmed to breed in large numbers, so if you give them the chance they will do their part!

When to start using your insects

Do not be too quick to start feeding your insects to your animals after setting up your feeder colony. There is often a critical mass needed to keep a colony going. If you use the insects too soon or when the numbers are too low, then you risk the colony dying out or being unsustainable. The required critical mass varies by insect type and by the conditions they are being kept in.

Trial and error is needed and there will be a balancing act between running out and being overrun. If you experience the latter you know you are doing things correctly; you might advertise your surplus or swap some for different food types.

The choice of feeder insects included in this book is based on those most commonly available and easily bred. Only true insects are included. Once you have gained experience with one species of a given type, you may want to experiment with others.

Allergies

Some people can develop allergies to certain feeder insects and this is often exacerbated over time due to repetitive cleaning out or handling. This situation is uncommon but some insects are more likely to cause allergies than others.

Locusts are reported to be the worst culprits and after several years of breeding them I developed a rash on my arms that appeared immediately I cleaned out the locust cages. On some occasions the allergy would be sufficiently severe that I would need anti-histamine tablets.

Crickets and cockroaches have also been reported as causing allergies but to a lesser extent

These reactions are not common and should not be a concern when starting out. If any sign of an allergy is noted then medical attention and advice should be sought.

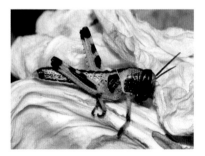

Locusts are notorious for causing allergies. Fortunately, for most people this is not a problem.

Crickets

Introduction

Crickets are members of the family Gryllidae and are related to grasshoppers and katydids. There are about 900 species of cricket in the world and they are all nocturnal.

In the wild, crickets are omnivorous scavengers, feeding on organic materials, including decaying plant matter but they will also eat dead insects, animals and a wide range of other materials. If there are no other sources of food available crickets will eat their own dead or even weakened crickets.

Crickets are easily obtained from pet shops (or on-line) in most countries. Because it is a cheap food source and readily available many people do not bother to breed their own. It can be an interesting exercise to breed a few generations but whether it is worth the effort in the long term will be a personal decision.

There are good reasons for breeding your own crickets. One motivation is the quality of the crickets you can feed to your pet. In some countries there have been problems with crickets carrying disease that may harm your animal or that have been bred in unhygienic conditions. This is more of an issue for the mantis keeper, as poorly kept crickets have been blamed for 'Black Death' in mantis.

A further consideration is the nutritional value of commercially produced crickets. This cannot always be assured, so the only way to ensure the highest quality is to breed your own.

Another reason is that occasionally there are market shortages of crickets.

If you decide to 'have a go' then you will need to maintain a good routine of cleaning out the cages. Food should be replaced regularly and dead crickets removed daily if possible. This is not an insect that can be left untended for long periods without unpleasant consequences!

Species

There are four species of cricket commonly sold in pet shops as food. These are:

Black cricket *Gryllus bimaculatus* – a larger species and, as the name suggests, black in colour. The exoskeleton is thicker, causing some to feel that it is not as easily digested as other species. They can be more aggressive than smaller species. On the plus side, they accept lower temperatures.

Brown or House cricket *Acheta domestica* – a species commonly used for food. The adult males can be noisy.

Silent cricket *Gryllus assimilis* – also a common food species. Silent crickets are not completely silent but are quieter than Brown crickets.

Banded cricket *Gryllodes sigillatus* – these look like a slightly smaller Brown cricket with black bands around the abdomen. They are more agile than the other species and can jump higher, making escape a potential issue, if not housed securely.

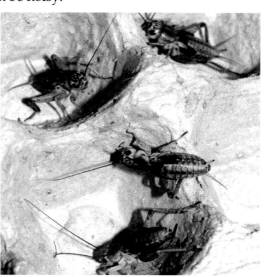

Silent Crickets *Gryllus assimilis*

Each of these species has its own advantages and disadvantages. The choice is a personal one but I prefer to use Silent crickets for feeding chameleons and mantis. The conditions for breeding all four species are the same and are discussed below.

Life Cycle

Crickets go through three stages of metamorphosis – eggs, nymphs and adults.

One female can lay several hundred eggs, depending on species and conditions, which may take between seven and ten days to hatch. The resulting nymphs undergo eight or more skin changes until they reach adulthood. This period may take between six to ten weeks, but is subject to temperature and food.

Adults are sexually dimorphic, with both sexes carrying wings. The males of most species can make considerable noise through stridulating, rubbing two specialised wing parts together (and not by rubbing

its legs together). The female is easily identified as she normally has a fatter abdomen than the male and will have a long needle-like ovipositor with which to push the eggs into the substrate or laying medium.

It is unlikely that adults will live more than four weeks.

Crickets dusted with calcium powder

Housing

There are many types of container that can be used but the main criteria are that it is large and secure. Crickets are good at escaping but cannot climb smooth surfaces well.

Crickets have a tendency towards cannibalism even when there is ample food available, with larger ones preying on smaller ones. Therefore, the faster growing nymphs are best housed together in a separate container away from their smaller siblings. This will help to manage the growing population but it will also prevent the cannibalistic adults eating the hatchlings. In addition, it allows for the different climate requirements needed for the various stages.

A plastic storage bin of 80 litres is ideal for the initial breeding container. Small holes, less than 1cm (0.4") should be drilled in the lid to allow for good ventilation. As this may allow smaller crickets to escape, it would be even better to make a couple of openings about 10cm (4") square in the lid and cover them with metal gauze hot-glued in place. If the container is kept too humid, the bodies of any dead crickets may turn to mush and attract small flies. The smell will alert you to the problem!

No substrate should be used as the crickets will generate droppings and scatter bits of food. Substrate will make the container harder to clean. As the lifespan of the adults is only a few weeks, you will probably find a number of dead crickets in your colony due to old age and this does not necessarily reflect poor keeping conditions. Dead crickets should be removed as soon as possible.

Crickets are territorial and need places to hide. To allow for this I use egg box cartons. The best are the egg flats that would carry about twenty eggs. Three or four of these sheets can be stuck together using white glue. This will give a free standing block that works well as a hideaway for the adults.

Temperature

Adult crickets will tolerate a wide range of temperatures but to optimise their breeding cycle you need to keep them at around 25°C to 30°C (77°F - 86°F). Pinheads need a slightly lower temperature and higher humidity than adults.

Heating requirements depend on where you keep your crickets and the climate where you live. Ideally, they can be kept in your reptile/mantis/spider room which will probably be heated to a temperature close to that required by the crickets. If kept in an unheated room the cricket container may be too cold, in which case heating pads will need to be used.

Whether the heating pads are placed on the top, side or at the bottom of the cage is a matter of choice. Crickets will avidly chew on any wiring, so the pads should not be placed inside the container. If you opt for placing a pad below the container, you may need to raise the container off the heating pad slightly to avoid creating areas inside of extreme heat - hot spots - which will prove fatal to the crickets.

Lighting is not essential as crickets are nocturnal but some breeders give the crickets a day period using a lamp.

Feeding

Many cricket keepers give a diet consisting solely of carrots which appears, at first glance, to work well but this is not ideal as the crickets will not thrive nor are they are being 'gut-loaded' for optimal nutrition when used as food.

Typical cricket set-up

Crickets are naturally cannibalistic and territorial, so ensure that there is always plenty of food available to minimise this. Dead crickets should be removed as soon as possible from the container as other crickets will eat them, which could lead to disease.

As previously noted, crickets are omnivorous, therefore in addition to vegetable matter dry food should be included, such oats, bran, etc. For protein, fish flakes can be added but these can be expensive, so dry dog biscuits are a good alternative. Since you will be offering them to your insectivores it is worth investing in their food.

How you provide water is a matter of choice. Some breeders put a small, shallow tub in the cage with a piece of wet sponge or other absorbent material; others use water gel crystals. Do not use a container with just water alone as there is a risk of the crickets drowning.

As the crickets will clamber in and around the water container and foul it, it is important to change the water and clean the water container regularly.

An alternative is to provide 'wet' food such as carrots, potatoes or similar fruit and vegetables. The benefit of using these food items is that they increase the nutrition and hydration of the cricket.

Breeding

A minimum mix of 100 adult males and females will be required to start a breeding colony to allow for the possibility of a high mortality rate; 500 would be a better starting stock. It is easiest to tell the sexes apart when they are adult, at which stage the females have an ovipositor - a long, needle-like appendage, protruding from her rear. The males are slightly smaller and will be the ones making the noise.

Crickets breed readily, so pairings will not be a problem.

Egg laying

Egg laying is prolific but keeping the eggs safe requires preparation as these could be eaten by the adults.

First, a suitable medium is needed for the eggs to be laid in. The most common is a peat-based soil. Florist oasis and old carpet can also been used. Whichever you choose, it is best to fill a small plastic box about 10cm x 7.5cm x 5cm deep (4" x 3" x 2" deep).

Second, cover the egg-laying medium with plastic or metal netting that has a mesh size of about 5mm (0.2") or slightly less. The netting should be cut to fit the shape of the box and held in place by several elastic bands or hot-glued in such a way that no crickets can get between it and the egg-laying medium.

The laying medium should be damp, but not wet, and packed into the laying box so that when the netting is placed on top it is directly in contact with the medium.

The laying box is then placed in with the main colony of adults.

Females will lay many eggs in the medium, through the netting, but will be unable to burrow down and eat the eggs that have been laid.

Within a few days the laying box should contain hundreds of eggs, most laid about 2cm (0.8") below the surface. At this stage, the laying box should be removed, dated and replaced with a new one.

Care of eggs

Remove the protective netting from the laying box filled with eggs and place it inside a hatching box, which should have reasonable ventilation and a tight fitting lid. A 5 litre square box can be used but it needs to be plastic to avoid holes being chewed and deep enough that there is no risk of pinheads escaping.

The eggs are kept at the same temperature as the adults but not higher than 32°C (90°F). The atmosphere in the hatching box should be humid but not so damp that it encourages mould. If the egg-laying medium dries out it is likely that the eggs will die, so it is important to keep it moist. Light spraying from a spray bottle can be used if the medium is drying out.

Eggs will hatch between seven and ten days after being laid, subject to the temperature. Once the main hatching has occurred it is always worth keeping the laying box in the hatching box for another week, as some will hatch several days later than the others.

Care of pinheads

After the pinheads have hatched you can either use the hatching box as a rearing box or you can move the pinheads to a new container, the same size. The advantage of moving the pinheads is that later hatchings may be at risk of cannibalism from older crickets. The disadvantage is the risk of the small pinheads escaping during the transfer.

As their names suggests, pinheads are very small and easily overlooked. They like to stay hidden if given the chance, so sections of egg carton should be placed at the bottom of the rearing box. The pinheads will congregate under the carton making transfer easier. Keep the temperature lower than for the adults, at around 25°C (77°F), and the humidity slightly higher.

Offer your pinheads dried food crushed to a very fine powder. If 'wet' food is used it will need to be monitored closely as the more humid environment will encourage mould. When removing old pieces of fruit or vegetables check them carefully as the pinheads may burrow inside and you may be helping them escape.

Water is needed, as the pinheads will dehydrate quickly. Unfortunately, they have a tendency to drown even in a small drop of water! One option is to put wet cotton wool in a jar lid but not so wet it makes a puddle. This will allow the pinheads access to water with a lower risk of drowning. Regrettably, some will still succeed!

Some breeders use small sections of cardboard egg box soaked in water. This needs to be replaced daily as it dries out quickly and gets covered in droppings. I find this method better than cotton wool for providing water.

Excess humidity may result in droplets of condensation that will lead to drowning, so this should be monitored daily and additional ventilation provided if it becomes a problem.

Some pinheads will grow faster than others and may be cannibalistic. You may decide that this is an acceptable loss or you may wish to separate them once their size advantage is spotted.

The hatchlings can be kept in the rearing box until they are about half grown, after which they can be safely introduced in the breeding box of adults or used as food.

Related to crickets, katydids and grasshoppers are readily eaten by most insectivores. Compared to crickets, however, they are harder to breed in large numbers, making them impractical as a large quantity food source.

Caution

Crickets are masters of escape and hiding. In your pet's cage an un-eaten cricket can pose a serious risk to smaller animals at night, as the cricket will have no qualms about feeding on them. I once lost a large tarantula during a moult when it was attacked by crickets that had hidden in the substrate. If you are feeding pinheads to your chameleon hatchlings be aware that the crickets will grow faster than the chameleons and, if allowed to remain in the cage, they could soon pose a problem.

Breeding crickets can be time consuming but if a colony is being kept successfully the benefits of easy access to good quality adults and all sizes of nymphs, including pinheads, can be money saving and well worth the effort.

Crickets lay large numbers of eggs so, with the correct conditions, it is relatively easy to breed your own pin-heads.

Cockroaches

Introduction

Members of the order Blattodea, there are about 4,500 species of cockroach, which live in a wide range of environments around the world. Although considered pests associated with disease, there are only about 30 species that are commonly found in proximity with humans and, of these, only four are considered serious pests.

Cockroaches are mainly nocturnal and will normally try to avoid light. Although most species prefer warm climates, cockroaches are among the hardiest insects and can survive extremes at both end of the temperature scale. Some species are capable of remaining active for a month without food and are able to survive on very limited sustenance. They are omnivorous, feeding on organic materials, including decaying plant matter, but they will also eat dead insects and animals.

Compared to crickets, cockroaches have some advantages as feeder insects. They are unlikely to attack a small chameleon in the same way that a cricket might. They are longer lived and are hardier. Most are easier to breed than crickets and they make no noise! Unfortunately, despite these advantages, they are not as readily accepted by some animals as crickets are.

Cockroaches suffer from a perception they harbour disease and that they smell. The species shown below will not do so if kept in clean conditions and fed correctly.

For mantis, cockroaches can be a better choice than crickets. They are normally readily eaten and do not seem to carry the same risk of disease to mantis.

Male Turkestan *Shelfordella lateralis*

Species

There are around a dozen species of cockroach commonly being bred as food for reptiles and other insectivores. The most common of these species are:

Lobster roach - *Nauphoeta cinerea*
Dubia or Guyana Spotted roach - *Blaptica dubia*
Turkistan roach - *Shelfordella lateralis*
Madagascan Hissing roach - *Gromphradorhina portentosa*
Green Banana or Cuban roach - *Panchlora nivea*

The care and breeding of all the common species are virtually identical, so a general description of housing, food, etc., is given below. Any specific differences needed for a species are mentioned under its own subheading.

Most of the other species likely to be encountered will share the needs of one of these shown below. None of the pest species are covered and these should be avoided for health reasons.

Dubia roaches *Blaptica dubia*

Life Cycle

In most species there is a marked sexual dimorphism and the sexes can be differentiated prior to adulthood. The females normally produce a hardened egg case called an ootheca (from a Latinised form of two Greek words meaning 'egg' and 'covered' – covered egg). In some species the oothecae are dropped or laid, while in others they are carried inside the female until they hatch, making it appear that the youngsters are born live, without the egg stage.

One female may produce dozens of oothecae during her life and each ootheca may contain between 10 and 50 eggs depending on the species.

The hatchlings from an ootheca are referred to as nymphs. They will undergo several skin changes, typically between five and seven, until they become sub-adults and, finally, adults. Because the nymphs resemble adults in many ways this is called an incomplete metamorphosis.

The lifespan of cockroaches is subject to species and environment but most will live up to one year, although the Madagascan Hissing roach may live for three years or more.

Housing

With the exception of the Dubia and Turkestan roaches, most species can climb plastic (and glass) and can also run along the underneath of the lid, so any ventilation holes need to be covered in fine-wire mesh. A tight-fitting lid is also needed, not just to prevent escapes but to stop wild geckoes and other predators climbing into the box. Before I realised what was happening I lost several cockroaches to these unwanted visitors. As geckoes can crawl through very small gaps, I now use window/door foam draught excluder placed along the top edge of the container to keep them out.

As an extra protection against the risk of escapees a barrier can be made by rubbing a 8cm (3.1") wide band of Vaseline along the inside of the container just below the lid. Cockroaches are unable to get a grip on the petroleum jelly and cannot climb out. This method works well for nymphs but some adults can fly, so the lid will be needed as well. Vaseline has the disadvantage that it attracts dirt and needs removing and replacing every few months.

An alternative to Vaseline that can work well, although more expensive, is a Teflon-based paint sold in the States as Bug Stop specifically for painting around the top edges of cages to prevent insects climbing out. It is water-based, so can be damaged when cleaning

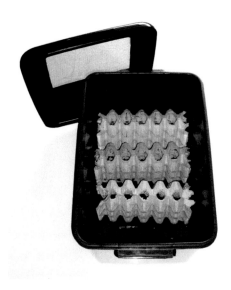

Box for cockroaches – also suitable for crickets

out the container and may require a touch-up.

The size of the containers needed to house the main breeding stock of cockroaches will vary depending on their adult size. For most species, any plastic box of between 25 litres and 80 litres will work well. Ventilation holes should be drilled in the lid or, preferably, openings about 10cm (4") square should be cut out and covered with a fine-wire mesh hot-glued in place. Madagascan Hissing roaches are best kept in 80 litre storage containers.

For all but the Green Banana roach no substrate is needed, as it makes cleaning difficult. Glue two egg flats together with white glue. These can stand on end and create a suitable hiding area. Several of these hiding areas can be used together and the number you will need depends on the size of the container and the number of roaches.

Temperature

All cockroaches will breed well at between 27°C and 32°C (80°F - 90°F) but some will breed faster at higher temperatures as detailed below.

Feeding

Cockroaches are remarkably easy to feed – they eat almost anything! However, to get the best results from your breeding efforts and to provide the best food for your insectivores more than dinner scraps are needed.

Aside from quantity, the food for all types of cockroaches will be similar. Due to the inevitable higher humidity in the container it is important that any food used, dry or 'wet', is monitored and removed if its shows signs of mould.

Dried dog food is a good source of protein and can be simply left in a corner of the cage; it is more readily eaten when it has been crushed to a powder. Fish flakes will also provide good protein but can be expensive and best used only for the nymphs. Other dried foods, like bran and oats, can be given but should be placed in a shallow feeding dish, such as a jar lid, which can be easily removed, cleaned and replaced, as the food is prone to going mouldy if it gets damp or contaminated with droppings.

If the diet regularly contains a good proportion of 'wet' food then it is unnecessary to provide water. I have never added water to the colonies of any species of cockroach I have bred. Water can be quickly fouled and may increase the risk of mould. If you want to put water in the cage, it is better to use water gel crystals. Alternatively, a shallow dish of water can be provided with cotton wool or a sponge in it to prevent drowning; this will need to be replaced regularly to stop bacteria and smell.

Ootheca and nymphs of the Turkestan roach *Shelfordella lateralis*

Breeding

Dubia or Guyana Spotted roach - *Blaptica dubia*

Dubia roaches are popular for the ease with which they breed and their relative longevity. Males can live for nine months but females will often live for double that. The adults are about 5cm (2") in length and males can be distinguished from the females by having wings.

Females will become mature at about six months old and from that time will produce roughly twenty to thirty 2.5mm (0.1") long white nymphs every month or so. These are produced ovovivoparitally, which means that the female lays an ootheca but then pulls it back in-side herself to incubate. This gives the appearance that the female is a live-bearer.

Female Dubia *Blaptica dubia*

The absence of exposed, laid oothecae has advantages to the hobbyist in that there is neither the need to set up hatching boxes nor any fear of the adults eating them, although there is little evidence of cannibalism among the species if they are kept well fed.

Males are territorial and too many males in a confined space can lead to fighting and reduced breeding. A ratio of one male to between three and five females is ideal; excess males can be fed to your reptiles or larger mantis.

Adults can climb plastic but not as successfully as some other species, making them less of an escape threat. Males can fly but not far nor without provocation.

Lobster roach - *Nauphoeta cinerea*

This species is often incorrectly listed as *Naupheta cinerea*. Also known as Speckled roaches or Woodies, adult Lobster roaches grow to 3cm or 4cm (1.2" to 1.6") long and both sexes live for about one year, maturing at around three to four months. At this age, the females will start to produce oothecae which they will retain inside themselves for roughly a month before producing 30 to 40 small nymphs. Like the Dubia roach, the young are produced ovovivoparitally, which gives the appearance that the female is a live-bearer.

Lobster Roach *Nauphoeta cinerea*

Unlike many cockroaches, Lobster roaches display no obvious sexual dimorphism and both sexes are winged. A comparison will show that the males are flatter in the body and have longer wings. The female's abdomen is more rounded than the males and for those with the patience and keen eyesight, females have two small white dots on the underside at the rear end of her abdomen. Most people start a colony with 50 to 100 roaches and assume that there will be an adequate distribution of sexes.

Lobster roaches can climb plastic and glass with ease, so a secure container is essential. This ability can make feeding them to your reptile a challenge, as they can disappear into the cage and hide at the bottom, unseen and thus uneaten. Despite having wings it is unlikely that they will use them to escape as they tend to flutter weakly rather than fly.

This species is popular because of its reputation for being one of the fastest breeders on the captive cockroach list. They thrive at the higher end of the temperature range and at 32°C (90°F) they will reproduce rapidly. Because of the speed at which the colony can grow it is important to plan ahead and ensure that they are not too crowded, as once they reach a critical mass they will start to die off rapidly.

Turkestan roach - *Shelfordella lateralis*

There is confusion about the correct name of this species and in the States it is commonly advertised as *Blatta lateralis* and can sometimes be found elsewhere as *Shelfordella tartara*. Even the common name can be confusing: Turkistan or Turkestan. I have opted for the spelling of the country.

Less commonly known as Rusty Reds, the Turkestan roach is my favourite feeder food not just for chameleons but also for mantis. They can't climb smooth plastic and the males rarely fly. They are active runners, which means they will attract the attention of chameleons and other reptiles

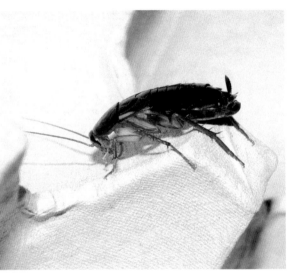

Female Turkestan *Shelfordella lateralis*

that rely on movement to sight their prey. Young nymphs can be a good food for small insectivores and pose no risk to them, unlike small crickets.

The adults are sexually dimorphic, with winged males and wingless females. The males are also a lighter brown-red colour than the females. They grow to about 2.5cm to 3cm (1" - 1.2") long and can live for up to one year. Both sexes mature at around three to five months and the females will then lay an ootheca every couple of weeks. Each ootheca may contain between 20 to 30 eggs. The oothecae take two to four weeks to hatch, subject to temperature. Some ootheca may take longer, so don't throw older ones away too quickly.

The oothecae are normally scattered about the container but can also be found hidden in depressions in the egg cartons. You can either leave them to hatch where they are or collect them for hatching in a different container. The advantage of using a hatching box is that you can monitor the growth of your colony more easily and you can keep the oothecae at a slightly higher humidity. If the humidity drops too low then oothecae may not hatch. Having the small nymphs in a separate container makes it easier to feed them to small insectivores as it removes the need to separate out the larger nymphs and adults each time you use them as food.

Turkestan roaches like a high temperature and anything between 30°C and 35°C (86°F - 95°) is ideal. If your colony is slow to get going or the number of oothecae seems fewer than expected, check that the temperature is not too low. Getting a colony thriving is not as easy as with some other species but once established the numbers increase rapidly.

Try to keep a ratio of one male to every four females, although this is not as critical as with Dubia roaches.

Madagascan Hissing roach – *Gromphradorhina portentosa*

At anything from 5cm to 10cm (2" - 4") in length, weighing up to 20 grams (0.7 ounces) when full grown and living for three years or longer, the Madagascan Hissing cockroach is an impressive insect.

It is easy to identify males as they have two large bumps on the top of the prothorax that some have likened to horns; these are called pronotal bumps. The males are also larger than the females. Neither sex has wings.

Madagascan Hissing roaches differ from the other roaches in this section not simply because they are bigger but also as this is the one species that is often bought and sold as a pet. This means that the cages they are kept in can range from utilitarian, plain plastic boxes with no substrate to ornamental showcases containing leaf mould, logs and plants. As we are concerned with breeding this species as a feeder insect we will focus on the former.

This species prefers temperatures in the range of 26°C to 35°C (79°F - 95°F), with a moderate humidity – don't keep them dry but be careful not to allow mould to grow.

Despite comments often made to the contrary, Madagascan Hissing roaches can tolerate lower temperatures. I once inadvertently placed a colony in the corner of our garage in the winter where it was forgotten and subjected to 10°C or 50°F (and lower) over a period of several weeks. The colony survived with minimal losses and started breeding again once the temperature was raised. I would not recommend such low temperatures but this shows how resilient some species can be.

If the roaches are not breeding, check that the temperature is not too low.

To have a good breeding colony you will need to use a plastic storage bin of about 80 litres capacity. Ventilation is important, as is a barrier of Vaseline or Bug Stop – all sizes can climb but the smaller nymphs can do so with ease.

The food and water requirements are the same as for other species. Mine only receive 'wet' food as the water source and thrive but some breeders use water crystals or even shallow dishes with wet cotton wool or sponge. Being larger, there is less risk of the nymphs drowning.

Madagascan Hissing roaches take about five months to mature.

Madagascan Hissing roach
Gromphradorbina portentosa

They are ovoviviparous, producing oothecae that hatch within the female's body making it appear as though this is a live-bearing species. The females will give birth to between 30 and 50 young every two months or so.

The males are territorial and defend their small territories by pushing rivals with their 'horns' and hissing. Females and nymphs can enter the defended territory without disturbance but rival males are attacked.

To create a successful breeding colony it is necessary to allow the males to have territories to defend. This can be done by placing blocks of egg flats in the cage. White-glue four or five flats together to make a block and stand the block on its end. Males will each find a part of the block they will defend, which will facilitate the breeding cycle.

The hissing sound is unique to Madagascan Hissing roaches as it is produced by forcing air through spiracles on the abdomen – other insects rub body parts together to make their sounds. The hissing sound can be made by nymphs of either sex from the fourth instar onward and can be a warning sound or, in the males, a challenge to fight.

This is an interesting species to keep in its own right. As a feeder insect it has the advantage of being large and popular with Parson's chameleons. Full-size adults might be a challenge even for larger reptiles but the nymphs are ideal for most animals.

Green Banana or Cuban roach - *Panchlora nivea*

The Green Banana roach is an interesting species to breed. Its requirements are slightly different to the other species but its green colouration and habit of flying makes it a good food item for chameleons and other active hunters. There are two types normally available – the standard one and a 'giant' form. Their needs are identical and some breeders keep both types together with no hybridisation.

This species is an expert at escaping: the adults will fly at the slightest provocation and they can climb fast on almost any surface. Smaller nymphs do not seem as good at climbing smooth surfaces and prefer to lurk in the substrate. Whether this ability to escape is a problem depends on where you live. In northern Europe, with its colder winter temperatures, it is very unlikely that any escapees would survive long enough to breed. Even in a heated house the humidity would be too low for an infestation. Other locations and climates may favour the roaches and would require a more carefully designed cage set-up to prevent escapees.

A smaller container is normally used for Green Banana roaches than for the larger species. A 5 litre plastic box would be sufficient for a small colony but double that size would be better. Its height needs to allow for a Vaseline barrier at the top edge but this will only stop the nymphs from escaping and not the adults.

Green Banana roaches *Panchlora nivea*
(photo by Virginia Cheeseman)

Green Banana roaches need a warm and humid environment with a soil substrate. Most people use coconut fibre or an open peat-based soil to a depth of about 5cm to 7.5cm (2" - 3"). Ventilation is needed, so small holes will need to be made in the lid. You may need to adjust the size or amount of the holes as there is a fine balance between allowing adequate ventilation and keeping the humidity high; if it becomes dry, the roaches will die. It is advisable to hot-glue fine wire gauze across holes in the lid to stop nymphs escaping.

Green Banana roaches like to hide, so part of the substrate should be covered. Inside the container egg flats are likely to get wet and go mouldy very quickly, so cork bark is a better choice. Simply placed on top of the substrate, it will provide a hiding place for adults and nymphs.

Males are about 15mm (0.6") long and females up to 25mm (1") in length; when adult the 'giant' form is roughly 25% bigger. The females are ovoviviparous, producing oothecae that hatch within their bodies making it appear as though this is a live-bearing species. Nymphs take between three and four months to mature. A female can produce about 30 nymphs at a time, every two months. The young nymphs are very small and quickly disappear into the substrate.

The roaches eat the normal cockroach foods already mentioned and will get enough water from the 'wet foods' described earlier. Put food in shallow dishes but only small amounts at a time as they do not eat much and the heat and humidity will make it go mouldy quickly. Remove all bad food; mould can kill the roaches. If you need to spray the substrate to increase the humidity the food dish should be removed first.

Tank cleaners like isopods or springtails (Collembola) can help to control mould without hurting the roaches. They will thrive in the damp substrate and feed on food scraps and droppings. They are not a substitute for good hygiene but will help.

Despite being unpopular when roaming free in the house, keeping cockroaches is a growing hobby in its own right and there are now many species being kept as pets and for study.

Caution

Some species of cockroaches don't move very much and others are quick to hide, so some predators simply ignore them. How well your animal accepts cockroaches will depend a great deal on how they are offered. If they are simply dropped into the cage, the cockroaches may quickly disappear from view but if the non-climbing species are put into a deep enough dish they will remain visible and are more likely eaten.

An infestation of escaped cockroaches will be viewed, perhaps unfairly, as a greater health hazard than crickets. Some species are also better escape artists than crickets, with the ability to fly, so you should use all possible precautions to avoid escapees.

At 8cm (3.1") long, this male Madagascan Hissing roach is an impressive insect. It's a great climber but unlikely to become a pest in temperate regions even if it escapes.

Lepidoptera

Introduction

Flying insects are particularly attractive as food to reptiles and mantis due to the movement they make. Butterflies are the ultimate flying food!

Offering butterflies and, to a lesser extent, moths can be a great way to encourage a 'bored' reptile to eat if it has been off its food. Moths may not be as mobile as butterflies and often quickly hide in the shadows, which can make them a less attractive option but still useful.

The obvious question is: - where to get the butterflies? Catching them in the wild is one way but it can be hard to find a regular supply due to the environment or changing seasons. In some areas there may also be legal or cultural restrictions that prevent this. Some people feel that with butterfly populations declining worldwide, catching them as food for pets is unethical. Breeding your own butterflies and moths may be the answer, providing you with a regular and reliable source of food.

The larvae of many butterflies and moths are attractive to most reptiles and mantis but these are normally even harder to find in the wild than the adult stages. Some larvae have protective spines or long hairs, which can make them unsuitable.

Butterfly larvae are fairly easy to rear but pairing the adults can be a challenge due to the need for sunlight,

Swallowtail Butterfly *Papilio multicaudata*

large cages that allow for flight and food plants, etc. For this reason moths have become the more popular source of food.

To add variety to the diet offered to my chameleons and mantis, occasionally I have caught individual female butterflies in the wild to obtain batches of eggs which I have then reared using the techniques discussed below.

Breeding butterflies and moths is a fascinating hobby in itself that can be time consuming. Many butterfly species only eat specific food plants and have exacting requirements, which is why the information shown below is only a brief summary of general Lepidoptera care. The Internet is a good source of information on the additional needs for a particular species if you wish to breed one of these.

Species

There are over 170,000 documented species of Lepidoptera found around the world, in all but the most inhospitable areas. The Arctic Apollo (*Parnassius arcticus*) survives even within the Arctic Circle.

With so many species, it is hardly surprising that many are bred by hobbyists. However, not all are suitable to breed for food as most are not easy to keep for multiple generations nor do they breed quickly enough to provide the numbers needed for food or in sufficient numbers to be of much use as food.

Some butterflies rely on certain poisons to protect themselves – Monarch butterflies (*Danaus plexippus*) are a well-known example. In most cases, a poisonous butterfly will advertise the fact by its colouring to warn

Leopard Butterfly larva *Phalanta phalantha*

birds and reptiles not to eat it. It is worth checking a reliable source, either books or the Internet, to make sure that the butterfly you are breeding does not carry toxins.

Mantis do not seem to be affected by these toxins but always check before feeding a Monarch butterfly to your prized *Toxodera*.

Cabbage White butterflies (*Pieris* species) breed quickly on easily obtained food but they are, like many species, prone to disease when the larvae are kept in crowded conditions, making them surprisingly difficult to keep over multiple generations.

Tomato and Tobacco Hornworms (*Manduca* species) are often sold as feeder foods but for breeding purposes are also notoriously hard to keep alive for multiple generations. If large numbers are required they need a lot of space – and a huge amount of food.

The two most commonly bred feeder species are described below. One is a pest and the other domesticated.

Life Cycle

The life cycle of Lepidoptera is well known – ova or egg, larva or caterpillar, pupa or chrysalis (sometimes within a cocoon) and, finally, imago or butterfly/moth. Most children have reared at least one species, either at home or at school.

The time taken to complete the life cycle can vary dramatically between different species, from as little as a few weeks for some to nearly a decade for others.

Eggs may hatch within a few days or can over-winter. Some larvae can increase in body mass 1,000 times during their life time!

Leopard Butterfly pupa *Phalanta phalantha*

Many moth larvae build cocoons in which to pupate; other moth larvae burrow underground and make silk-lined chambers. Butterfly larvae normally pupate in the open, hanging down or supported by a silk girdle.

The adults will often live for several weeks. Some species hibernate over winter, living six to eight months or more. *Heliconius* species from South America can live as adults for a similar period but remain active throughout, with no hibernation.

Some moth species, for example the silkmoth, do not feed as adults and these will have a shorter life span, often as little as one week.

Housing

Caterpillars or larvae can be kept in several ways:

The easiest and least time consuming method is to keep them on a growing food plant. You will need to surround the plant with a net cage to stop the larvae wandering off and to protect them from parasites. This can be done using a large 'sleeve' of netting that covers a branch, tied at both ends. Alternatively, if you are using a pot plant, the whole plant can be sleeved, with the net bag tied at the top and at the base of the plant. Alternatively, the whole potted plant can be placed inside a large, netting cage.

If the needed food plant is not in your garden or not practical to 'sleeve' you can cut branches and put them in a container of water inside a netting cage. It is important to plug the top of the water container as larvae may walk down the

Sleeving larvae on a living plant removes the need to keep changing the food.

branch into the water and drown. Check you are not cutting plants without permission. Some plants fare better than others when used as cut food. Sappy plants may wilt quickly but branches from trees and bushes can last several days before they need replacing.

Another method is to keep the larvae in air-tight plastic boxes. The box needs to be air-tight to keep the food fresh. There will be ample air inside the box for the larvae to survive for several days. Despite this, the box will need to be cleaned out every day to remove droppings or frass, and to avoid mould. Fresh food will need to be given daily. Ensure that the leaves used are dry, as any water will quickly increase the humidity.

If the box is not kept scrupulously clean it will not be long before disease is evident in your caterpillars. Some diseases can destroy a thriving colony within a single day. With good hygiene this can easily be avoided.

When the larva is large enough to pupate it may change colour and wander around its box or sleeve. It is best to remove it to a separate container so it can pupate in peace. If it is a moth species that makes cocoons, add a few leaves or crumpled sheets of paper to the pupation box. The cardboard tube from a toilet roll also works well. If it is a larva

that pupates underground then a large flowerpot filled to a depth of about 20cm (8") with clean compost should be provided.

Pupae can be laid out to hatch in a large netting cage, out of direct sunlight. Branches or twigs should be provided to allow the newly emerging adult to climb in order to hang down and complete its wing expansion. The pupae should be lightly sprayed with water every day but not drenched.

It is important to allow space for the wings to develop fully when hatching.

The wing cases of the pupa will darken a few days prior to hatching.

Some moths will mate in fairly small cages. Most butterflies require a large, airy, netting cage, placed in bright sunshine with ample nectar-bearing plants and caterpillar food plant on which to lay their eggs. Some species of butterfly need considerable room to allow for elaborate courtship flights. Not all do and some will pair in a cage about 1 metre (or 3 feet) cubed. These are the exceptions.

The size of the cage will vary by species but for the best results you might consider converting a greenhouse or glass house into a giant, walk-in cage.

The above information is, by necessity, brief and is designed to give a summary of what might be required for breeding many butterfly and moth species.

In contrast, the two feeder species described below are relatively simple to breed and do not take up much space. If the cages are kept clean, disease should not be a problem. The adults do not feed and re-quire minimal room for mating.

Temperature

With such a diverse range of species and habitats, it will be no sur-prise that the temperature requirements vary considerably between the many butterfly and moth species. It is especially complicated with spe-cies that over-winter and hibernate as eggs or larvae.

The two feeder species described below prefer similar temperatures of between 20°C and 28°C (68°F - 82°F).

Feeding

Caterpillars consume a huge amount of food during their develop-ment and many species are plant specific regarding what they will eat. These days it is possible to rear several species on artificial foods. Arti-ficial foods are often sold in powder form, which is then made into a paste and stored in the fridge until needed.

Making your own artificial food from scratch is complex and diffi-cult. The ingredients required, including a range of chemicals and antibiotics, can be hard to get. Absolute cleanliness is required at all stages of preparation to avoid contaminating and ruining the whole batch. The facilities needed are closer to those found in a laboratory than a kitchen.

Adults of butterflies and some moths like to feed on nectar, pollen or rotten fruit.

It is possible to substitute sugar water for nectar in many cases. To do this, mix a spoonful of sugar with enough hot water to fully dissolve it. Add a small amount of honey and mix in thoroughly. Place a wad of cotton wool into the solution to soak it up and become wet. When it has cooled down, place the butterfly on top, holding its wings closed. Too much honey will result in a shorter life span for the adult.

You may need to encourage the butterfly to feed by very gently using a pin to unroll its proboscis or tongue and carefully touching it to the wet cotton wool. Once it is feeding you can release your hold on the wings.

There are some beautiful butterflies in cultivation, such as this *Cethosia biblis*, but few can be bred in large numbers or are suitable as food items.

Breeding

Waxworms

A pest in beehives, waxworms are the larvae of one of two species of *Galleria*; the one most commonly bred for food is *Galleria mellonella*, the Greater Waxworm.

The larvae grow to 25mm (1") and are taken with gusto by most reptiles. The moths are also taken by chameleons and mantis but care is needed to prevent them escaping if they are not eaten immediately; they can become pests in the house. Waxworms are rich in fat and make an excellent treat but should be used with restraint due to their high fat content.

Waxworms can be bred easily in large numbers – each female may lay thousands of eggs.

Very important is the use of an escape-proof container. The larvae can eat through netting, some plastics, paper and many other materials - including prized books, expensive carpets and favourite clothes. As they are great escape artists, a secure glass, metal or hard plastic container is needed to prevent such damage.

The larvae generate a large amount of heat as they eat and grow, far more than you would expect from a bug. This heat will cause moisture to evaporate from the food, which may then condense on the sides of the container and run back into the food, turning it into a slimy green mess within days, killing your colony.

Waxworm colony, showing clumps of cocoons

To prevent this, allow for good ventilation as the larvae grow larger. This may mean using a 25 litre box, depending on the number of larvae you are raising. A good way to ensure good ventilation is to cut out holes about 10cm (4") square from the lid and hot-glue a very fine metal mesh over the holes. The size and number of holes will be found with experience.

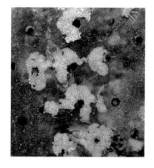

Waxworm eggs

To avoid the problems of heat generation, it is sensible to split your colonies frequently to keep the number of larvae per container low. If not overcrowded, a 5 litre container, with ventilation holes cut and covered with mesh, should suffice.

There are many good recipes for waxworm food on the Internet but the simplest is to dribble some honey on a Weetabix and briefly microwave it, so that the honey soaks in. This is not as nutritious as some recipes but it is quick. If you decide to use one of the Internet recipes, you will often find that beeswax is an ingredient. This can be bought relatively cheaply at most health food shops.

The life cycle is greatly affected by temperature. At 28°C (82°F) the whole cycle could take as little as seven weeks but at 20°C (68°F) it will take much longer.

Once the larvae pupate, leave them alone and the moths will emerge in a few days. They mate easily and the females like to lay their minute, yellow eggs in crevices, such as around the lid of the container. If you crumple some wax paper and put it in with the female moths you will find rafts of eggs in the folds. Once the eggs turn pink you know they are fertile and they should hatch in about four days. Don't expect to see the newly hatched larvae – they are very small. It may be a week or two before you are even aware that the next generation is present.

A common complaint about breeding waxworms is the amount of silk thread they produce. Larger larvae build tough cocoons which tend to clump together, making it hard to get at them.

The least dangerous way to prevent the silk production is to subject the adult larvae to extreme cold. Put them in the freezer for between 5 and 20 minutes – the timing varies a great deal due to many factors, so you will need to experiment to get it right for your situation. Only try a few larvae initially until you are satisfied that you have found the right timing.

Waxworm box, with fine mesh in the lid

Several other options have been suggested, including dunking the larvae in various chemical solutions, which has obvious risks both to the waxworm and the eventual eater of the waxworm.

Commercially produced waxworms, bought from pet shops, do not produce the copious and annoying amounts of silk but the next generation will do unless treated. I have never found it a big problem and do not try to stop the silk production.

Silkworms

Silkworms (*Bombyx mori*) and their moths are a superb addition to the insectivore's diet. They are more nutritious than crickets and are readily taken. With the use of artificial food it is now possible to breed silkmoths throughout the year. Silkworms (the larval form or caterpillar of the silkmoth) have the added advantage that they can survive for a few days in the insectivore's cage, even without food, and cause no damage to the cage or the animal.

Due to the lack of a chitinous exo-skeleton, silkworms cannot be used exclusively as food because doing so might risk causing digestive tract problems in your animal.

However, when used in conjunction with crickets or cockroaches they make a nutritious and welcome addition to the regular diet.

Silkworms need to be kept clean, well-ventilated, and not over-crowded. Several diseases can wipe out a colony of silkworms in one or two days. (While we may associate Louis Pasteur with his work on immunisation and pasteurisation, it was his work combating silkworm diseases that saved the French silk industry in the mid-19th century.)

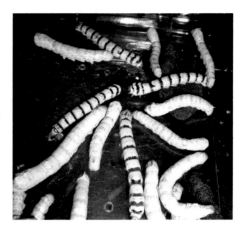

Silkworms can be striped or plain – they are still the same species.

The only natural food on which the larvae thrive is mulberry leaves, which can be a problem as mulberry trees are not easily found in many countries. Various other plants are touted as an alternative, such as beetroot, but only mulberry will consistently keep the larvae alive and well through to pupation.

The single dependable alternative to mulberry is artificial silkworm food, often sold as a powder. This is made into a paste, which is then kept in the fridge until needed. Many generations can be successfully reared on artificial food.

Fresh mulberry and artificial food can be combined to keep down costs. However, be aware that silkworms will switch from artificial food to mulberry easily but sometimes they are reluctant to change the other way around.

There are several types of artificial food available but the most reliable originate in China. The Internet shows suppliers in Europe and the U.S. but most of these import from China and redistribute. Buying from them may be more convenient than dealing directly with the manufacturer as generally they will only sell in large quantities.

Using artificial food is obviously more expensive than mulberry but it has been observed that the larvae often grow faster and bigger on

Silkworms feeding on artificial food.

artificial food than they do on mulberry leaves, with less disease evident. If you use artificial food, cleanliness is vital to avoid mould on the food.

Do not use too much artificial food at one time as it can quickly go mouldy if there is excess moisture. Put in just enough with the silkworms so it is completely eaten by the next cleaning out time.

If you are buying livestock over the Internet it is likely that you will opt to buy eggs, which are cheaper and often more easily available. There are several strains available, relating to the quality of silk, colour of the larvae and the number of broods each year.

So far as the larval colouring is concerned, there is no difference between the normal white larvae and the so-called 'zebra' silkworm. They both produce normal silkmoths and neither type grows bigger nor faster than the other. It is a simple colour variation.

If you want to have greater control over your silkworms numbers you should opt for a single-brooded strain. This may sound strange when multi-brooded strains are available but you cannot control the timing of egg hatching with these so easily and may be overwhelmed by the number of small larvae. On the other hand, by using a single-brooded strain it is possible to store surplus eggs in the fridge for many months until they are needed.

The life cycle of the silkmoth follows that of all Lepidoptera – egg, larva, pupa and adult. With a single-brooded strain the overwintering stage is the egg. If left alone, the eggs will remain dormant for about nine months. After the dormancy, the larvae hatch and consume vast amounts of food becoming full grown larvae within six to twelve weeks (subject to temperature).

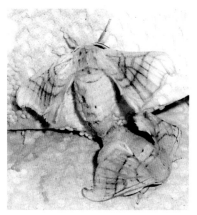

Silkmoths cannot fly and need no special conditions to mate. This female started to lay her yellow eggs but the male mated with her a second time, showing the need to remove the males as soon as they have finished pairing.

The silkworms then make the cocoons for which they are famous and inside these they pupate. If you have several silkworms about to pupate at the same time it is wise to put the mature larvae in their own cardboard tube to pupate; this avoids having a tangle of cocoons. The cardboard tube from inside a toilet roll works well.

Roughly two weeks later the moth emerges. The moth cannot feed or fly. Its sole purpose is to mate and for the female to lay between 100 and 250 eggs. A male will normally die within three to six days of hatching, depending on whether it has mated. Females may live for a week or slightly longer.

The differences in the sexes is obvious, with the female having a large abdomen filled with eggs and the male having heavily pectinate (feathery) antennae. The male's forewings are also more hooked at the tips than the females.

Mating is certain if a

Male Silkmoth

male and female are near each other. They will pair for about 24 hours and once they separate it is best to remove the male, otherwise he will continue to attempt to re-mate with the female, stopping her from laying eggs.

Moths of both sexes are readily eaten by insectivores.

The mated female will normally lay her eggs on the cocoon from which she hatched. However, this is not the best option if you plan to store them in the fridge. To make matters easier, remove the mated female from the cocoon as soon as she separates from the male, or both of them even while still mating, and put her/them in a plastic tub (about 10cm/ 4" in diameter) lined with kitchen paper towel. She will lay her eggs on the paper and it becomes a simple matter to store them in a container in the fridge.

The eggs are yellow when first laid but soon become dark if fertile. Leave them for about two weeks after laying before storing them in the fridge. The fridge should be at the normal chilling temperature and no colder – do not use the freezer!

Keep the eggs in the fridge for fourteen weeks. At the end of that period you can take out as many as you want, leaving the rest in the fridge – if they were laid on paper it will be easy to cut off the amount required. Between one and two weeks after removing the eggs from the fridge the larvae will hatch.

The rest of the eggs should remain viable in the fridge for around nine months; some will hatch even after a year but the numbers successfully hatching will be reduced. Once you get a colony going you can have silkworms as a food source throughout the year.

Silkmoth eggs taken from the fridge.

Caution

Waxworms are very fatty and eaten with enthusiasm by all reptiles. This can be useful if you are building up a gravid female or a weak male but be careful not to over feed them on waxworms.

Waxworms are masters of escape. They can become a pest in the house during the summer.

Silkworms are also eaten readily and can provide a highly nutritious treat but without a hard exoskeleton too many silkworms on their own can create digestive problems. This is easily remedied by alternating between crickets/cockroaches and silkworms.

Silkworms can be a nutritious and regular food for reptiles, if part of a balanced diet.

Diptera

Introduction

Due to their active movements, large house flies are attractive to many types of reptile, amphibian and mantis. In the summer, it is normally easy to catch many flies, sometimes more than you would like! Unfortunately, their availability can be unreliable, especially as the weather cools. Fruit flies are also often annoyingly common but equally unpredictable.

Another problem with wild-caught flies is that you do not know where they have been feeding. By their very nature, house flies favour rotting meat or faecal matter, which may lead to disease either for the insectivore or for the owner.

In some countries it is easy to buy both maggots and fruit flies over the Internet and this may be a good option, given some of the problems associated with breeding them.

In other countries, however, it is not possible to buy either maggots or fruit flies, so if you plan to rear animals that need Diptera, for example chameleon hatchlings or mantis nymphs, you will need to breed your own.

It is worth noting that a lack of fruit flies has been the cause of several failures in breeding chameleons for the pet trade in South Africa over the recent years.

Mantis (*Harpagomantis tricolour*) eating a house fly. Many species of mantis are reported to need flying insects to produce good ootheca.

Species

True flies, Diptera, are distinguished by only having two flight wings, hence its name 'Di' meaning two, 'ptera' meaning wing. They have two other wings, which are less obvious and called halteres. There are about 240,000 species of Diptera which includes mosquitoes and gnats, as well as 'normal' flies.

You will encounter many species of fly as you pursue your hobby – carrion flies, coffin flies, lesser house flies, etc. Most of these are worthless as feeder foods and difficult to maintain in colonies, despite their pest-like appearance.

Soldier flies, *Hermetia* species, are often sold under the name Phoenix fly. They can be a useful source of food, both as maggots and as adults. Rearing the maggots to get adult flies is simply a matter of providing rotten fruit and having patience.

In warmer climates, it is easy to attract adult Soldier flies with rotten fruit (mango seems best in my opinion). Soon large numbers of maggots will be available for food. Breeding the adults is not an easy task and the complexities involved put this species outside the scope of this book.

Life Cycle

Flies undergo complete metamorphosis. The female fly lays her eggs close to or on the larval food. After a few days the larvae or maggots hatch and start to feed. They will grow rapidly, often together with large concentrations of other maggots, changing skin as they grow. Maggots do not have legs and are thinner at the mouth end. After completing its growth, a full-grown maggot will wander away from the food source to pupate, normally in drier conditions.

The adult fly emerges from the pupa and the cycle starts again. Some species of fly will overwinter in the adult form.

Breeding

The culture and breeding requirements of the two main types of fly kept as feeder foods differ so greatly in almost every aspect they will be considered separately.

House Flies

Introduction

House flies can be a valuable food source for many insectivores. Certain mantis species thrive on house flies but do not so well if fed crickets.

Breeding house flies is not for the faint-hearted. At first glance you may think that it would be easy but there are some interesting challenges in captivity, not least of which may be resistance from other members of the household.

Carrying over a hundred possible pathogens, it is important that the highest standards of hygiene are maintained at all times when breeding house flies.

It is a good idea to conduct any breeding experiments with flies in a shed or garage away from the home. This is to avoid the inevitable re-criminations when the presence of escapees is discovered in the kitchen. Another reason for keeping fly breeding off-site is the smell, as maggots produce a sharp tang of ammonia if not managed carefully.

The eggs and maggots need to be kept damp, whereas the pupae and adults require a drier environment.

Species

The common house fly is *Musca domestica* but there are several species used as feeder foods that often come under the heading of house flies. These include various blowflies, such as the Bluebottle, *Calliphora vomitoria*, and the Greenbottle, *Lucilia sericata*. Commercially sold maggots will normally be one of the blowfly species.

A variation that has become popular recently is the Curly Winged Fly or Terfly. This results from a genetic mutation in the normal house fly, *Musca domestica*, in which the adult has under-developed wings and cannot fly. These are bred using exactly the same conditions as house flies. A proportion of the adults will be normal, winged flies. These must be removed quickly or else they will mate with the less dominant wingless type, causing the whole colony to ultimately revert to its flying form.

Life Cycle

The length of time for each stage varies greatly, subject to temperature. Each female will lay several batches of between 100 and 150 eggs in her life. Eggs can hatch in as little as eight hours.

The resulting maggots moult three times and then, prior to pupation, change colour from white to pink. The larval or maggot stage will normally take about two weeks. If allowed to, the pupating maggot can wander a considerable distance before finding the ideal spot to change.

House fly maggots feeding on dog food.

After two to six days the house fly hatches and the cycle starts again. In optimum conditions the whole cycle from egg to adult could be as fast as seven days but three weeks is more normal.

Housing

It is important to realise that the conditions needed for each stage of development are different and that the whole cycle cannot be accomplished in one container.

Eggs and younger maggots require a more humid environment than older ones. As the older maggots get closer to pupation they will try to escape to a drier area and will often swarm away from the food. The pupae need to be kept dry.

Feeding

Adult flies need to drink water as well as eat. Damp sugar makes a good food for the flies but spraying with water is also necessary.

The choice of food given to the maggots will determine your success rate and the strength of the smell given off. It may also affect the potential risk of introducing disease, not just to your pet but to yourself.

There are dry recipes that can be found on the Internet that claim to reduce the smell. One such recipe is:

1 part coarse wheat bran

1 part dry milk powder

1 part plain flour

Enough water to make a doughy mixture

A certain amount of experimentation is needed to get the mix and the conditions right but the key issue is not to make the mixture too wet. Be prepared for failure initially, possible unpleasant smells and perhaps unkind comments from your family! But persevere and these minor setbacks should pass.

A simpler way to feed the maggots is to use small chunks of tinned dog food. I have used this method and have had no problems with smell, as long as only enough food is given to the maggots that can be eaten by the end of the day.

Temperature

Adults should be kept at around 25°C (77°F). Maggots will tolerate a much wider range of temperatures and generate heat themselves when crowded. If they are also kept at 25°C (77°F) they will thrive; the hotter they are kept the faster they will develop, peaking at around 30°C (86°F).

Adults will tolerate very low temperatures and can be stored for days in a fridge (not a freezer) whereas maggots can survive for weeks at such temperatures.

Breeding

In captivity the easiest way to get the flies to lay eggs is to use a shallow dish, such as the lid of a jar, into which several layers of folded tissue are placed. Pour fresh milk over this until the tissue is damp and leave it in the cage with the flies. As the milk turns sour the flies will lay their eggs on the tissue.

Once several rafts of eggs have been laid, the laying dish is removed and placed in a rearing container and another dish put in its place. This way several rearing containers can be started.

House fly eggs laid on an old, cooked chicken. Rafts of 100 or more eggs can be laid at a time, with several hundred laid during the fly's life.

Do not leave the laying dish in with the adult flies for too long before removing them, as the maggots may hatch after only eight hours. If any egg rafts have been laid away from the laying dish, it is possible to use tweezers to carefully lift them and place them in the rearing container.

I use two different sized rearing containers during the maggot growing phase. A small plastic box about 10cm (4") square is used for the egg and small maggots.

As the eggs will probably be several hours old before you remove them, when you place a 1.5cm (0.5") cube of tinned dog food next to the eggs you will soon see lots of minute maggots crawling on the food. Add more food each day but be careful not to overfeed to avoid smells. Initially, you can keep the lid on the container to prevent maggots from escaping but once they have grown a little the amount of ammonia they produce can kill them if there is no fresh air circulation.

As soon as the ammonia smell indicates that they need more ventilation, I move them to a tall plastic sweet jar with a square of ladies' tights held in place over the opening with rubber bands. This not only allows for ventilation but is also to prevent other insects entering, rather than the maggots escaping. With its soft body, a maggot can squeeze through virtually any opening, including the mesh of tights.

If the maggots are too crowded or if the atmosphere in the container becomes too humid, they will teem up the sides. To prevent excess dampness I add digestive bran or sawdust to the jar. The maggots will also swarm when they are ready to pupate.

If the maggots do start to swarm up the sides of the jar to pupate, which is often indicated by an early change of colour, I place the jar in a large bowl filled to a depth of about 2.5cm (1") with digestive bran or sawdust. The maggots will pupate in the dry substrate and not wander any further.

It is possible to store the pupae for some time in the fridge to slow down the hatching and to enable you to manage the number of flies you have at any one time.

Handling Flies

Catching the flies to use as food can be a challenge even when they are contained.

There are two ways I do this. The first is to separate as many pupae as you need as flies per day into a plastic box with a lid. The pupae can be put to one side to hatch or kept in the fridge to slow their development. Once they hatch the container, complete with flies, is put in the fridge for five to ten minutes which will stun the flies.

The stunned flies can be placed in your animal's cage with minimal risk of them flying off initially. Once they warm up, they will quickly become mobile again.

The second way I catch the flies is to adapt a large plastic jar by cutting a hole in the side large enough to allow me to put my hand through. A wide plastic cylinder is then hot-glued into the hole. Attached to the outer end of the cylinder by rubber bands is a 15cm (6") length from the leg of a pair of ladies tights, from which the foot has been cut off, creating a tube. This allows me to put my hand through the tights into the cage with little risk of the flies escaping when I am changing the laying dish or catching flies to feed my animals.

Flies will always go towards light, so aiming a spotlight at the side of the cage away from the opening will draw the flies to that side, making them easier to catch. I use small plastic boxes with lids to catch the flies but any small container with a lid will do. If the room is bright, then the side of the cage away

Even with elaborate cages, some escaped flies will still be found around the house.

from the light will need to be covered to make it dark.

It is possible to store the hatched flies in the fridge for several days. When kept in the fridge the flies become torpid and can easily be removed, dusted with vitamin powder. They will soon warm up and become active, ready for feeding to your animals.

Obtaining Flies

In some countries, e.g. UK and the US, it is possible to buy maggots from a fishing shop. They will often be coloured to make them more attractive as fish bait. As far as I can determine in the UK the colouring is harmless. I have fed coloured maggots to praying mantis with no ill-effects.

Maggots bought from a shop are normally full grown and require no food as they will be close to pupation. They can be kept for several weeks in the fridge. Squats are smaller maggots that still require growth before they pupate; they are not so commonly seen in fishing shops.

In countries where it is not possible to buy maggots, another way to start your fly culture is to place the remains of a cooked chicken carcass outside where neither birds nor pets can get at it. So long as the weather is not too cold, this will attract flies and within a day or so you should find rafts of white eggs inside the rib cage and you can continue as above.

Caution

When breeding flies it is imperative that extremely good hygiene is maintained at all times – hands should be regularly washed and all containers thoroughly cleaned. Never use old meat or dead animals as food for the maggots as this will increase the risk of disease to your pets and yourself. There is a chance of botulism if insufficient caution is exercised.

But do not be put off - many people safely rear thousands of flies each year.

Fruit Flies

Introduction

Fruit flies are an essential food for newly hatched chameleons, mantis nymphs and many smaller lizards and frogs. In most countries, if you leave a lump of banana lying around during the summer you will get lots of fruit flies. These flying wild ones are not as easy to feed to your animals as the cultivated flightless varieties.

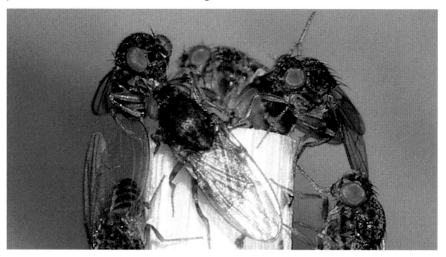

Flightless fruit fly *Drosophila hydei*

Species

There are several flightless species in cultivation but only two are commonly available: *Drosophila melanogaster* is the most well known and comes in two forms – vestigial winged and wingless. *Drosophila hydei* is a larger, fully winged fly with red eyes but also without the ability to fly.

Life Cycle

Fruit flies go through the same cycle as house flies – eggs, maggots (larvae), pupae and adult flies. Typically, the whole cycle will take about 14 days, although *Drosophila hydei* can take a few days longer at the same temperatures.

Housing

The simplest container is a 500 ml (0.75 pint) plastic cup with a paper tissue held across the top by a small rubber band. This allows for some ventilation without letting wild flies in. Fine netting has the disadvantage it can allow wild fruit flies in to breed with your flightless stock and degrade it. Once that has happened you will need to start from scratch.

Flightless fruit fly culture

Unlike house flies, all stages of fruit flies can be kept together in the same container.

The food mixture is put on the bottom of the container to a depth of about 2.5cm (1"). Above that either a small ball of plastic straw, ornamental straw, broken wooden skewers or even upturned (unused) coffee filters is placed. This is necessary to stop the adults drowning and to provide a drier place for the larvae to pupate.

Cleaning the containers between cycles is important but hot soapy water is sufficient if rinsed thoroughly.

Feeding

There are numerous recipes on the Internet for breeding fruit flies. For example:

250 ml (1 cup) instant potato powder
125 ml (1/2 cup) powdered milk
60 ml (1/4 cup) white sugar
A pinch of brewer's yeast

Common to these recipes typically are brewer's yeast, sugar and some sort of binding agent, such as instant potato powder or flakes, corn flour or oatmeal. Some, such as the Carolina Mix, are marketed under a brand name.

When I first started breeding fruit flies I used a variation of the recipe shown above and, while it and most of the others worked well, I found that it involved more time and effort than I could give. I often had over 100 cultures running at any one time and could not boil, mix and stir enough of these 'complex' mixtures to keep up.

The food I find best is simply mashed banana mixed with enough coarse digestive bran to make it into a stiff paste. Nothing else is added. I tried a little yeast initially but found that it made no obvious difference.

With the mix of banana and bran I have been able to keep cultures of both types of fruit fly running for several years. The fruit flies reared on this mixture supported many generations of Veiled, Panther and Carpet chameleon hatchlings and my surplus pots of fruit flies were sold in South Africa to keepers of chameleons, dart frogs and other pets.

Some experimentation will be needed to get the mix of banana and bran right – overnight the banana will normally start to ferment and become quite liquid but adding too much bran will cause the mix to dry out before the fruit fly cycle is complete. You will soon find a happy balance and your efforts will be rewarded with cups of swarming fruit flies.

Temperature

Both species of fruit fly do well at temperatures ranging from 22°C to 28°C (72°F - 82°F). Warmer temperatures can help to increase production but excessive warmth will cause sterility among the flies and the culture will die out. Conversely, temperatures below about 20°C (68°F) will slow production noticeably, although such low temperatures usually will not kill the flies.

Breeding

Tip a large number of fruit flies into the cup once it has been pre-pared as described above; about 100 to 150 is a good number if you can count them! Be quick to cover the top of the cup with tissue secured with a rubber band as the fruit flies will quickly climb up the inside of the cup and escape. It may be necessary to bang the cup on a hard sur-face to knock them back down.

In less than a week you should see small maggots in the mixture. The adult flies will continue to lay eggs even while the first maggots are growing. After a while, the number of adults will have dropped off dramatically but by then the maggot population should be large.

A few days later small, light brown cylindrical pupae will appear on the sides of the cup and about two weeks after starting your culture you should see the sides of the container almost black with newly hatched flies. Take what you need for feeding but keep enough back to start a new culture.

By continuously starting new cultures in clean pots with fresh food you will avoid problems with mites and the unpleasant smell that comes from an old banana mixture.

If the mixture looks like it is drying out before the flies have hatched, simply drop in a dollop of mashed banana. You will quickly see the maggots swarm up to it.

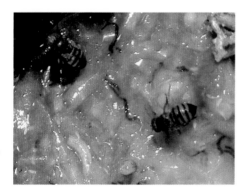

Drosophila melanogaster, the Wing-less fruit fly, is smaller than *D. hydei* but make excellent food for smaller animals.

Feeding Fruit Flies to your animal

It is easy to feed fruit flies to your pet: put a small plastic container that has been half filled with mashed banana into the animal's cage and place a small upright stick in the banana, such as the end of a wooden skewer or a toothpick - but remember to remove the sharp end. Tip in some flies and they will soon find their way to the end of the stick where they will be eagerly eaten. Fruit flies are not particularly nutritious so dusting them with a vitamin supplement can be advantageous.

To make handling easier, it is possible to knock some fruit flies from the breeding cup into a plastic container, put the lid on and place the container in the fridge. Five minutes in the cold will normally be sufficient to stun them. Once removed from the fridge, they will quickly warm up and become active again. Even if the fruit flies have been forgotten in the fridge for several hours and appear lifeless, leave them to warm up before deciding if they are dead.

Caution

Mould

Many of the recipes found on the Internet include some form of mould inhibitor. This is normally methylparaben, a well-known antifungal agent (E number E218). In Europe, this is frequently marketed under the name Nipagin, while in the US the name Tegosept is more often seen.

At very high concentrations Nipagin can damage the fruit fly culture by slowing the growth rate, so follow the instructions carefully. It is unlikely that you will cause any problems for your reptiles if you use methylparaben as it is a naturally occurring chemical in many fruits.

I tried Nipagin for a while but found no great benefit in its use. Occasionally, one culture will exhibit mould but it is usually an isolated case and does not warrant the expense of using Nipagin. Other recipes suggest using apple cider vinegar as a mould inhibitor.

If you do get black mould in your culture something is very wrong and the culture, flies, etc., should be disposed of. Green or blue moulds are not normally a problem in small amounts.

Mites

As each culture matures, start a new one or else small mites will appear and slow the breeding of the flies. Initially, these mites are very hard to see with the naked eye and are often present in low numbers. Unfortunately, the mite numbers can rapidly rise to the extent that they can cause cultures to crash completely.

By starting new cultures regularly and keeping the area where the containers are housed clean you can minimise the problem. Some breeders recommend the use of anti-mite paper, which is usually sold in rolls. By placing your containers on top of a sheet it should prevent the spread of mites.

Fruit flies are prolific breeders when given the chance

Beetles

Introduction

Beetles are members of the order Coleoptera, which make up a staggering 25% of all known life forms on the planet! It is an incredibly diverse order, with species found in all parts of the world except the Polar Regions. Some are agricultural pests, others pollinators, many are carrion feeders, while others can dispose of dung with ease – the almost limitless breadth of habitat and diet is amazing. They range in size from a few millimetres to giants over 15 cm (6") long.

Among such a variety of types and sizes, it comes as no surprise that some make excellent food for captive insectivores. As a food source beetle grubs are highly nutritious, comparable to silkworms.

Coleoptera is Greek for 'sheathed-wing' and it is the hard wing cases, or elytra, that make the adults less useful for food. Grubs, however, are normally edible and readily taken by chameleons and many other lizards. If the right species is chosen, and the correct conditions provided, they are among the easiest of the feeder insects to breed, requiring little maintenance or daily care.

Species

About 450,000 species have been named to date, with many more awaiting classification. Of these only a few are economically viable as feeder food. In most cases, it is the grubs that are used and not the adults.

Species that are useful as feeder insects need to have a relatively short life cycle, easily obtained food and no natural defence mechanisms, such as large jaws on the grubs or chemical sprays.

Mostly, this restricts the choice to chafers of the Cetoniinae subfamily, sometimes also known as Fruit Beetles, and mealworms of the Tenebrioninae subfamily. Grubs of other species can be used but either the larval development is very slow or the grub is too valuable to beetle enthusiasts to use as food.

Life Cycle

All beetles undergo all four stages of metamorphosis: egg, larva, pupa and adult. The larvae are normally called grubs.

Depending on the species, females may lay between a few dozen and a thousand eggs during her life time.

Grubs of African Rhino beetle (*Oryctes*)

The grub hatches from the egg and increases dramatically in size before pupating. The species we are concerned with in this book normally grow rapidly but even some Fruit Beetle species can take several years to complete their larval stage. When fully grown the grub will pupate, often in a cocoon or pupal chamber, usually made of mud or debris.

Weeks or months after pupation the adult beetle will hatch and the cycle starts again. In many species, the newly hatched beetle will remain inside the pupal chamber for a few days before emerging. A few species may remain inside the pupal chamber until some external factor, such as rain, encourages them to emerge, which may be weeks after they have hatched.

In some species, if the grubs are overcrowded or short of food they can become cannibalistic. If adequate food is provided this will not be a problem and the grubs can be kept together in one box. Always check first, as some grubs are not just cannibalistic but carnivorous.

Breeding

The requirements of Fruit Beetles and mealworms are very different in all stages of their development, so they are considered separately below:

Fruit Beetles

Introduction

Many people breed Fruit Beetles as a hobby in itself and there are forums and websites providing a great deal of information on the different species.

The larvae of some Fruit Beetle species can be very saleable, making it more economic to breed them and sell them as grubs than to feed them to your pet!

Unlike mealworms, Fruit Beetle grubs have a leathery rather than chitinous skin, which makes them a better food source. They are readily taken by most reptiles; avidly by some.

Species

There are, perhaps, 4,000 species of Fruit Beetle or Cetoniinae. These range in size from small to very large, as in the case of the aptly named Goliath beetle (*Goliathus* genus). The grubs of the Goliath are carnivorous and require specialised care, making them unsuitable as food.

Pachnoda beetles feeding on rose flowers in South Africa.

Other species of Fruit Beetle are very colourful and quite large, such as *Chelorrhina polyphemus* and *Dicronorrhina derbayana*. Although these are relatively easy to breed, they can take a year or more to complete their life cycle, which makes them less useful as a feeder insect. The majority of non-carnivorous Cetoniinae can be reared easily using the following method. Even so, with such a wide variety available, check if the one you are breeding has species-specific requirements, either for egg laying or temperatures.

The most common Fruit Beetles bred for food are members of the *Pachnoda* genus, often known as Sun beetles or Fruit Chafers. The majority of these species come from Africa and the two most commonly kept in cultivation are *Pachnoda sinuata* and *Pachnoda marginata*, which require similar conditions.

In South Africa, *Pachnoda sinuata* is common on the Highveld and is a pest of commercially grown roses, where the adults feed on the flowers.

Life Cycle

As with all beetles, Pachnoda beetles start as eggs, develop as grubs, pupate and emerge as adults.

Pachnoda beetle grub

The life cycle can take from two to six months depending on the conditions. Grubs will moult three times. Many adults may live for several months after emerging.

Except for the adults, all of the life cycle takes place underground. When fully grown the grub will make a hard cocoon chamber out of the surrounding compost. Inside the cocoon chamber it will pupate and complete its metamorphosis. After the adult has hatched it will remain inside the pupal chamber for several days until its wing cases are fully hardened.

Housing

The following description is for setting up a container for housing grubs, which is the most common way that Pachnoda beetles are bought. There is no difference between this set-up and the one for breeding the adult beetles except for the compression of the soil as described below under Breeding.

Because the majority of the life cycle takes place underground, containers large enough to hold about 20cm (8") depth of soil are needed, with a gap between the top of the compost and the lid of about 10cm (4").

Adult beetles are good flyers, so any container should have a secure lid. A 25 litre plastic box, with a lid, should be adequate. It is possible to use a smaller box but it is not advisable. If you have space for an 80 litre plastic storage box, so much the better.

Box for beetle grubs

Sufficient holes about 1cm (0.4") diameter should be drilled in the lid to allow for good ventilation and to permit light for the adults. However, it is preferable to cut out an opening at least 10cm to 15cm (4" - 6") square in the lid, which then has plastic netting hot-glued in place. If you are breeding larger beetles, you may need to use fine-mesh wire netting, as the adults can rip their way through plastic netting.

The soil needs to be slightly moist, so condensation will be a problem if there is insufficient ventilation. If the soil becomes wet at the surface due to excess condensation you risk an invasion of compost flies. These are harmless but annoying.

Add some rotten branches to the top of the compost mix to give the beetles something to hold onto after they have hatched. Just laying the branches across the surface of the soil will be sufficient.

Bear in mind that the container, when loaded with compost, will be heavy. Consider positioning the container where it will be kept before preparing it, as moving it later may be difficult and could even damage the plastic box.

With the container set up and in the desired position, simply add the grubs and wait. They will quickly disappear into the compost, out of sight. Except for checking that the soil is neither too dry nor too wet, at this stage you can more or less forget the grubs for a month or so. After that, check every few days until you see adult beetles wandering around the surface.

With the passage of time you will see that the compost changes texture as the grubs eat it. When it has become a fine tilth it is time to add more compost or leaf mould.

Periodically, start a new container to ensure that the compost is fresh and to prevent a build-up of mites or compost flies. Neither pest should become a problem unless the soil is kept overly moist or excess fruit has been put into the box for adults and remained uneaten after being pulled into the compost by the grubs.

Feeding

The grubs feed on rotting organic material and soil, so the compost in the container needs to be of good nutritional quality, as it will be the food for the grubs.

You can use waste food stuffs from your kitchen that has been composted but you must be careful to avoid non-organic items. Alternatively, you can buy bags of organic compost from a garden centre. Ensure that it is pesticide and fertiliser free.

Add a mix of leaf litter and rotting wood to the compost. The best places to get these are woods and forests of deciduous trees. Rotting leaf litter from the previous year is preferred.

The wood should be rotten enough to crumble easily and the best is normally white in colour. Break it into pieces about 1cm (0.4") in diameter or less. If you can break it into even smaller pieces by rubbing it between your palms, then it is suitably rotten.

The process of breaking up the rotten wood may create lots of fine wood powder, so you may want to use a face mask as it might contain fungal spores.

Never use coniferous wood, eucalyptus or yew. It will kill your beetle grubs.

A ratio of two parts compost to one part leaf litter and one part crumbled rotten wood is good but the ratio does not have to be exact.

The adult beetles feed on fruit. For a medium-sized population, half an apple laid on top of the soil every few days will be sufficient to feed the beetles. It is unnecessary to put the apple or other fruit into a lid or pot as it will soon rot down and add nutrients to the compost.

The adults will feed on many types of fruit including apples, oranges, bananas, etc. It is possible to buy beetle fruit jelly to feed them. Note that the jellies can attract ants and fruit flies.

In warm weather, or if you are over-feeding, you may find that fruit flies will come to the fruit if it is allowed to rot before it is eaten. If this causes a problem you can simply reduce the amount or change the fruit daily to stop the fruit flies breeding. Once your beetle colony is thriving, you will probably find that the fruit disappears into the compost mix as larger grubs pull it down to feed on it.

Temperature

Pachnoda beetles will survive at any temperature between 20°C and 32°C (68°F - 90°F) but thrive better in captivity around 25°C (77°F).

Breeding

In the wild, Pachnoda beetles are diurnal, flying on sunny days, so it is important to replace a segment of the lid with netting as described

Pachnoda beetle pupal chamber, opened to reveal pupa

earlier to allow for light to stimulate the adults to fly.

If you have males and females in your container mating is fairly assured. This will normally take place on the surface of the compost, often on the branches provided.

If you are starting off a new container for breeding purposes, then fill the container to a depth of about 10cm (4") with slightly moist compost, mixed as described above, and press down hard.

Very hard. It is unlikely that you will compress it too hard for the beetles!

On top of this compressed layer add the rest of your compost mix to a total depth of about 20cm (8"). Press that down fairly firmly.

Once mated, the female will spend increasingly longer periods underground, tunnelling to the bottom of the container to lay her small white eggs. The purpose of compressing the soil is that it allows her to make small egg chambers which are less susceptible to cannibalism by larger grubs.

Pachnoda beetles are strong flyers and may escape when the lid is removed if you are not careful.

It is best not to dig about in the soil to see what is happening. It is very tempting to do so but you stand a good chance of damaging the grubs or cocoon chambers.

Roughly two months after your beetles have hatched and been active you should have dozens of small white grubs burrowing in the compost. Subject to the quality of your compost the beetle grubs will grow at an amazing rate and soon you will have grubs up to 5cm (2") long, depending on the species. I have not seen any cannibalistic tendencies in this species, except for possible egg predation, and have kept hundreds of grubs in the same 80 litre container without problems.

There are many species of flower beetle kept in cultivation, such as this *Dicronorrhina derbayana layardi* found in South Africa. Most species have life cycles of a year or more, making them unsuitable as food items.

Caution

Normally, only first and second instar Pachnoda grubs are used for food. The mouth parts are very strong and third instar grubs could harm the intended eater.

When handled, Pachnoda grubs often void a black liquid but this is harmless. When the reptile chews on the grub some of this dark liquid escapes, which may look unpleasant but is normal.

Adults of some beetle species have the ability to spray toxic or noxious chemicals and should be avoided. Pachnoda beetles do not.

Some beetle grubs, such as this *Dynastes hercules*, grow to an enormous size. Species such as this will be worth more as live beetles than food. They can also bite!

Mealworms

Introduction

Mealworms are the grubs of Darkling or Flour beetles, a common pest in human foodstuffs, and members of the *Tenebrioninae* subfamily.

Species

There are two species of mealworm commonly available as food for insectivores: ordinary mealworms, *Tenebrio molitor*, and the superworms or King mealworms, *Zophobas morio*.

There can be confusion over the names and you may find ordinary mealworms, *Tenebrio molitor*, sold as Giant mealworms and occasionally see superworms, *Zophobas morio*, also sold as Giant mealworms!

Superworms *Zophobas morio*

Life Cycle

The life cycle of ordinary mealworms is standard for beetles and all four stages can take place in the same container. Mealworms can go through their complete life cycle in as little as five weeks but two to three months is more normal.

Superworms will take longer, anything from six months to more than a year. This is partly because they grow larger but also that they require specific pupation conditions that, if not met, will slow down the cycle considerably.

Housing

Almost any plastic container with a lid, with some ventilation holes in it, will suffice for the complete life cycle of ordinary mealworms. It is unnecessary to cover the holes with mesh, as neither the adult beetles nor the mealworms will climb the sides.

Superworms need a larger container, along with small pots for the full-grown grubs to pupate in. Superworms dislike daylight, so avoid transparent containers. Their container should be about 15cm (6") or more deep, with a gap of at least 7.5cm (3") between the top of the substrate and the lid. Good ventilation is important for both species.

The small pots for the full-grown superworm grubs to pupate in should be opaque and roughly 3cm (1.2") diameter by 6cm (2.4") tall and have a lid with some small holes for ventilation. It will contain only one superworm, so the size is not critical.

Feeding

Wheat bran or oat bran is commonly used as food. Some breeders add extra ingredients such as milk powder and crushed dog pellets, etc., for protein.

The food should be about 3cm (1.2") deep in the container for both types of mealworms.

Moisture is essential for the grubs. This can be provided by adding slices of 'wet' food such as carrot, potato and other vegetables or fruit. Because of the water content, the 'wet' food can make the bran wet and may encourage mould, so it is important to monitor it carefully.

One way to avoid the vegetables fouling the bran is to put them on some cloth, laid on the bran.

If insufficient moisture is provided, superworms will either eat each other or die off quickly.

Temperature

Ordinary mealworms are happy at room temperature but will tolerate a range between 15°C and 30°C (60°F - 86°F). Superworms cannot thrive in such a wide temperature range and will not survive below 20°C (68°F) or above 32°C (90°F) for long periods. Try to keep superworms between 22°C and 26°C (72°F - 79°F).

Breeding

Ordinary mealworms will breed readily. They require little maintenance except for feeding and an occasional clean out to remove the frass or droppings. Ordinary mealworms tolerate crowded conditions with little consequence.

Superworms, on the other hand, present certain complications. They dislike crowded conditions, so keep the population density low. Even when they are kept at a low density, the majority of the grubs will not pupate. This can lead to grubs living for many months and eventually dying without pupating. To prevent this, it is necessary to isolate the largest grubs in small pots as mentioned above. Pupation can now be controlled more easily and is more likely to occur.

Mealworm beetles *Tenebrio molitor*

At roughly four months old and about 4cm to 5cm (1.75" - 2") in length, the superworms can be isolated for pupation. They should be kept dark and without food. Between two and three weeks later they will probably have pupated. The pupa can be collected when hardened and put into a larger plastic box to hatch and later breed.

About two weeks later the beetle will hatch; initially it will be light coloured but will soon darken as the elytra harden.

To breed superworms, a separate hatching/breeding box is required. Although this is same size as the rearing box, it is necessary to prevent large superworms disturbing the pupae.

Just as with the rearing container, the breeding box for the super-worm beetles should have a layer of about 3cm (1.2") of oat bran or wheat bran on the bottom. A 10cm (4") square of egg carton will provide a place for the beetles to congregate when they have hatched.

Mealworm pupae *Tenebrio molitor*

If you have male and female superworm beetles, mating is assured. It is important to provide moisture for the adults or they will feed on the eggs. This can be provided, as for the grubs, in the form of carrots or other vegetables.

The female superworm beetle lays hundreds of eggs, which will take about two weeks to hatch. The eggs and the newly hatched grubs are very small, so it is likely that you will not see anything moving for a month or so.

It is advisable to remove the superworm beetles after four weeks and start a new colony in a new breeding box to avoid cannibalism by the adults on the small grubs.

Caution

Most insectivores, for example hedgehogs, birds, scorpions, and fish, benefit from the addition of mealworms to their diet. However, ordinary mealworms, especially older ones, should be avoided as food for reptiles as they have limited relevant nutritional value and a lot of indigestible chitin.

Superworms are more nutritious and have some value when it comes to feeding an insectivore that is reluctant to eat. However, they are often eaten with such enthusiasm that healthier food, with a better calcium content or nutritional value, may be ignored.

I feed neither type of mealworm to my chameleons for the reasons stated above but my mantis are fed on superworms and my water scorpions (Nepidae) avidly eat ordinary mealworms.

Superworms can be an ideal treat due to their high fat content but check their nutritional value for your insectivore.

Some smaller insectivores are reported to have had problems with superworms biting them. This does not seem to be a common problem, nonetheless some keepers recommend nipping the heads before using them as food for spiderlings and hedgehogs.

In some countries it is relatively easy to find flower beetles. Breeding your own grubs prevents putting pressure on the local population and should give you year-round access.

Locusts

Introduction

Locusts are a good food for many reptiles as they are large, nutritious and are quickly identified by the insectivore as something good to eat. It is unusual for a chameleon to refuse a locust, even if it has been fussy about its food previously.

Potential problems are that locusts are not always easily available in every country and can be expensive when they are. Breeding your own locusts is not as simple as some other insects but it is not difficult, if you can provide the right conditions.

Species

Although there are many species of locust, the two most commonly bred as feeder food are the Desert Locust, *Schistocerca gregaria,* and, less commonly, the Migratory Locust, *Locusta migratoria.*

The Desert Locust is infamous for its plagues across Africa and parts of Asia.

The Migratory Locust is far more widespread, found from Africa down to New Zealand. It can also swarm but the last major plague recorded was in 1942.

Life Cycle

Locusts start as orange eggs laid underground. They hatch in about one week as small black versions of the adults, called hoppers. Over the next six to eight weeks the hopper will change skin five times, becoming more like the adult each time. The final skin change will produce the winged adult.

If locusts are available for sale, then it is often possible to buy them either as hoppers of varying size or as adults.

Locust hopper

The life span is about three months but they can live as long as six months, subject to conditions.

Locusts occur naturally in two forms – swarming and solitary. There are differences in colour and behaviour between the solitary form and the gregarious or swarming form. Swarming locusts are often smaller and more yellow. It is the density of the population that normally controls which form is present and for mass breeding the swarming form is required.

Housing

Success with locusts requires a different set-up than for crickets and cockroaches. Rather than a plastic box, a more elaborate cage is needed for the adults.

For breeding, and larger hoppers, I prefer wooden cages 60cm high by 40cm wide and long (24" high x 15" x 15"). If you can provide bigger cages, so much the better. Some breeders have used old aquariums with wire mesh lids. Others have had success with Exo-terras but ventilation may be a problem with these, creating a damp environment.

Any form of netting cage is useless as locusts can chew through the netting.

Locusts need bright light to be active and a defined daylight period to breed. Subject to the type of cage you use, a light bulb will need to be fitted to the inside of the cage and connected to a timing device to control the daylight hours. If it is a tungsten bulb then it will have the added advantage of

Locust cage, with bottom drawer open

raising the temperature during the day.

Because locusts also need high temperatures at night when the light is off, thermostatically controlled heating will need to be provided.

The sides of the cage should be wire mesh to allow for ventilation. Locusts can chew through plastic mesh with ease, even when they are small hoppers. The combined need for ventilation and high temperatures can be hard to achieve. I adapted an old cupboard, which I insulated and heated, inside of which I kept two large locust cages. This enabled me to have greater control over the environment, without the need to place heating inside the cages

It is good to have sticks or doweling in the cage, angled at about 45°; this allows the hoppers to change skin more easily.

To make cleaning easier, inside each cage I made a false bottom of wire mesh with 1cm (0.4") holes. Below that was a sliding drawer as seen in the photograph. All the droppings and smaller waste fell through the wire mesh into the drawer and was easily removed by emptying the drawer. The mesh floor stopped the locusts escaping while the drawer was open.

Locusts are good at escaping and are fast movers. The doors of my cages are hinged but I also hang strips of plastic netting inside the cage, directly behind each of the doors, which acts as a secondary barrier. This allows me to put food or egg-laying boxes in the cage with no losses.

Feeding

Locusts will eat vast amounts when breeding. Cabbage or any other leafy green can be used, as can large-leaf plants from the garden – I use large quantities of Canna leaves (*Canna* species).

Coarse digestive bran is a good additive to put in a bowl in the cage.

Locusts get all the water needs from the fresh greens.

Temperature

Maintaining a high temperature is critical for the successful breeding of locusts. The cage needs to be kept at a minimum of 30°C. Ideally the daytime temperatures should be between 35°C to 38°C (95°F -

100°F). If they are kept at temperatures lower than 30°C (86°F) breeding will slow down to the point of being almost worthless; below 25°C (77°F) it will stop altogether.

The cage should be kept as dry possible because high humidity will destroy the colony. This is why at least two sides of the cage should be wire mesh to allow for adequate ventilation. If possible, all four sides should be wire mesh.

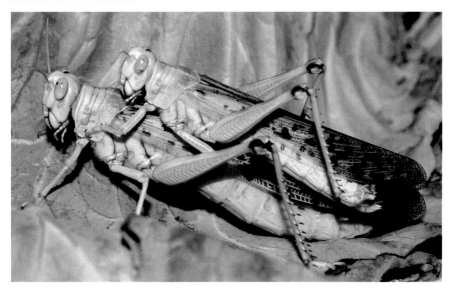
Male and female Locusts *Schistocerca gregaria*

Breeding

Before discussing breeding locusts, it is important to re-emphasize the need for high temperatures. Without them all attempts will fail.

To obtain your initial stock you can buy adults or hoppers. It is best to buy enough to make them feel crowded, so they breed well. The size of your cage will determine how many enough is.

The smaller male is yellow in colour, whereas the female is browner. They will mate freely about two weeks after their final moult if the conditions are right. The male will be seen sitting on top of the female with his abdomen bent under to meet hers. You may often see the male just sitting on the back of the female without mating when she is preparing to lay eggs.

A few days after mating the female look for a suitable place where she can lay her eggs underground. To provide such a spot fill a container with clean, damp sand. The sand should be damp enough that if you push you finger into it, the hole remains but not so wet that water will run out

Locust laying eggs

if you tilt the container on its side. A small hole in the base will allow any excess water to drain off. Any container that is about 10cm (4") deep will do - 5 litre plastic boxes are ideal. Put this in the cage.

The sand must be kept damp from the time it is placed in the breeding cage until the hoppers have finished hatching. This often requires daily additions of small amounts of water if the environment is as dry as it should be.

The female will push her abdomen deep into the sand to lay her eggs; it is amazing how far she can extend her abdomen to lay eggs. The orange eggs are laid in batches which are contained in a froth to provide the correct humidity. They are still susceptible to both drying out and over wetting, so care is needed. She may lay up to 100 eggs at a time.

From the first time you see evidence of egg laying wait about one week and then replace the box with a new one and move the old egg-laying box to the 'nursery' cage.

Care of the eggs and hoppers

Small hoppers are very quick and very mobile. If they are kept in the same cage as the adults, it will be harder to clean out the cage as the hoppers can drop through the mesh floor. It is easier to remove the egg-laying boxes and place them somewhere you can manage them more easily.

You can use a large plastic box as a nursery container. Initially, it does not have to be as well-ventilated as the adults' cage but should have adequate holes to prevent condensation caused by the droppings. Any ventilation holes drilled into or squares cut out of the lid should be covered in fine wire mesh. A 25 litre box should suffice. Put the egg-laying box inside and close the lid. Check daily that the sand is not too dry. Keep the box at the same temperature as the adults.

The eggs should hatch in about 7 days and, if all goes well, your nursery container will have hundreds of hoppers leaping about in it. Feed them the same food as the adults. After ten days or so they should be large enough to transfer safely to the larger wooden cages containing the adults.

Be careful of overcrowding the hoppers or else the accumulation of droppings may cause condensation issues. If this happens, move them to the bigger cages earlier or split them into other nursery containers. Every transfer of hoppers comes with the risk of some escaping.

I have found the best way to catch the hoppers for transferring them is to put the whole nursery container into a flexarium or similar large netting cage. Then carefully catch a few

Hoppers hatching

at a time in a plastic box, opening the zip or door just enough for the purpose. Do not leave the hoppers overnight in the flexarium or any netting cage. They will chew through it.

Caution

Strangely, the allergens from locusts have more effect on people than those from most other insects. Adverse reactions can be severe, involving rashes, eye irritation, breathing difficulties, even asthma attacks.

Keep the cages and the surrounding area as clean and as dust free as possible. Wash your hands thoroughly after cleaning out the cage or handling the locusts and wear a face mask if you think you may be at risk. Some literature puts the risk of allergy for those breeding locusts as high as 30%!

But to see a chameleon that has been on hunger strike rush forward to eat a locust makes the hard work worthwhile!

Mantis

Introduction

It may seem incongruous to include praying mantis as a food item in a book that may be used by mantis enthusiasts but some members of suborder Mantodea can be a useful addition to the herpetologist's larder. The adults, being high on the food chain, have good nutritional value. Newly hatched nymphs are very active and ideal for smaller insectivores, especially young reptiles.

These insects can be fairly time consuming to rear from eggs to adults. However, they are fascinating to keep and worth the effort, even if you find that you can't bring yourself to feed them to your reptile! You will soon see why there is such a large and growing interest in these creatures.

Mantis are good food items not only because they are active and nutritious but also because they can stay alive in the insectivore cage for several days. If other insects are available in the cage, such as crickets, it is possible the mantis will eat these and roam the cage for many days – if it isn't eaten first by the insectivore.

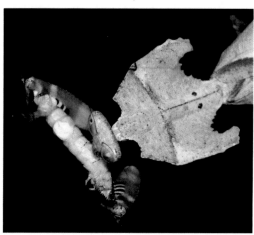

Dead Leaf mantis *Deroplatys dessicata* eating a mealworm.

With smaller reptiles or smaller chameleon species, such as *Brookesia*, first or second instar nymphs are ideal. They are very active and even a sluggish chameleon will move around the cage to catch them. Attach the ootheca to the side of the cage containing the young animal and let the ootheca hatch normally. There are likely to be fruit flies in the cage already for the young insectivore or chameleon to eat and the mantis nymphs will feed on these until becoming food themselves.

In warmer climates, it is possible to find mantis oothecae on fences or near windows where the females have been attracted by light. However, with many species it is only the males that are attracted to light.

In the States, oothecae can be bought from some garden centres as a form of eco-friendly pest control.

Female *Cilnia humeralis* mantis

Alternatively, search the Internet for suppliers. eBay is a good source and often cheaper than specialised mantis forums.

What follow is, by necessity, only an overview on how to rear and breed mantis. It is a diverse group, with many species that require specific conditions. However, these are unlikely to be bred as feeder foods.

This section is called Mantis and refers to species of the suborder Mantodea. Whether you use the word 'mantis' or 'mantids' is, to a great extent, a personal choice. The plural can also vary depending on where you live; you may see articles referring to 'mantis', 'mantises' or 'mantids'. According to the Oxford Dictionary 'mantis' is acceptable for both singular and plural and is the word I am familiar with and have used throughout this book. Other dictionaries differ!

Species

There are over 2,000 recognised species in 15 different families, which are broken down into about 430 genera. Among these species is a staggering diversity of shape and size. Some are so well camouflaged that they are useless as food, because your pet would never see them! Others are large and aggressive, willing and able to defend themselves against all but the largest lizard. I have seen a *Cilnia humeralis* female stand her ground in front of a large Veiled chameleon, displaying her warning colours. The bravado worked and the chameleon retreated, leaving her alone!

Among the best mantis to breed as food items are the commoner green species, such as *Mantis religiosa*, and the various *Sphrodomantis*, *Hierodula* and *Tenodera* species. These are fairly active and, being green, more attractive to the feeder. Fortunately, they are among the easier species to breed.

Others that are often available to buy can be more expensive, such as Dead Leaf Mantis (*Deroplatys* species), Ghost Mantis (*Phyllocrania paradoxa*) and Stick Mantis (*Popa spurca*). This makes them impractical as food but the requirements described below will still apply. Should you choose to breed them, Violin Mantis (*Gongylus gongylodes*) are also fairly easy to rear and breed, but worth too much to the hobbyist to be used as food. The conditions needed for this species are similar to the rest, with any major difference noted below.

Life Cycle

A female can lay up to 200 eggs at one time (less in some species), around which she produces a 'froth'. This hardens and provides protection against the climate and parasites. Each species has a distinctive shape and design for its ootheca, the name for the hardened egg case. A female can lay several oothecae during her lifetime.

Between four weeks and six months later the nymphs will hatch. The timing depends on species and temperature; most of the warmer climate species take between four and eight weeks.

The nymphs typically hatch all in one go but in some species the hatching is staggered over several days or even longer. Once the nymphs are free of the ootheca, they disperse to avoid attracting predators. In some species it is also to avoid cannibalism from their siblings.

Not all species are aggressively cannibalistic – some are fairly social

Many species of mantis show signs of cannibalism. The larger *Tenodera* nymph has started to eat its sibling.

and can be kept together until adulthood. It is worth checking the eating and social habits of the species you are keeping. Even known cannibalistic species, such as *Cilnia*, can be kept together for the first two instars with only minimal losses if enough food is available.

The number of skin changes varies by species and by sex, with females often having one or two more skin changes than the males, but typically it is between five and seven.

After the final moult the wings, if present, will be fully formed and the adults will start feeding heavily to prepare for mating.

Housing

Mantis cages can be as basic or as elaborate as you want. Mostly, it is wise not to use the same cage throughout the life cycle. Nymphs are better kept in smaller cages, so that the conditions and feeding can be controlled more easily.

The normally recommended cage size for larger nymphs is one that is at least three times as high as the mantis is long; this is to allow it to hang down when changing its skin. The width of the cage should be at least twice the mantis' length.

I have used 500 ml (0.75 pint) plastic cups for individual nymphs when breeding large numbers. The top of the cup is covered with a paper tissue, which is held in place by a rubber band. This allows some ventilation but, more importantly, it gives something for the nymph to hold onto when it moults.

As the nymph grows, the size of the cup may need to be increased to 1 litre (1.75 pints).

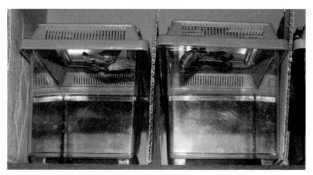

Plastic mini-pet aquariums can be used if you have lots of mantis. Cardboard screens will stop aggression between neighbours.

For larger nymphs and adults a bigger cage is required. Good ventilation is needed, so netting on at least two sides of the cage is ideal. Alternatively, you can use plastic mini-pet aquariums. A medium-sized Exo-terra can make a nice cage for large adults, especially more communal species like *Gongylus*. Additional lighting is not essential for most species and the normal lighting in a room should suffice.

Whatever you use, the cage should be escape-proof. Not only can mantis escape with more skill than you might expect but any food not eaten immediately may also escape and quickly become a nuisance.

Some people add substrate to assist in keeping the humidity in the cage higher. This substrate can be paper tissue, vermiculite or peat. Often this is more of an aesthetic addition than a necessary one as substrate can make cleaning out the cage difficult. Regular spraying with water should be enough.

The addition of live plants or even branches and twigs can be useful, especially during moulting time.

A different style of cage is often useful when pairing mantis, as discussed below.

Feeding

Mantis are predators and need live insect food. The food should be an appropriate size for the mantis – fruit flies are ideal for hatchlings and smaller nymphs, while house flies can be fed to larger nymphs and many adults.

Crickets can also be used for many species, although you will see many web sites saying crickets are bad for mantis. I have reared hundreds of individuals of many species very successfully on good quality crickets.

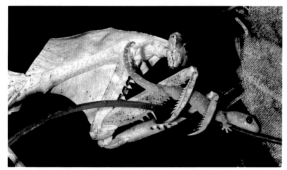

Mantis are ferocious predators. This young gecko wandered into the mantis cage looking for insects to eat but ended up eaten by one instead.

The crickets I used in South Africa were from a supplier that was very reliable and known for his clean stock. On the other hand, 'dirty' crickets were directly responsible for the death of a dozen of my *Deroplatys* (Dead Leaf mantis) when I first moved to Malaysia. So, if you are going to use crickets, check the cleanliness of your supply carefully. Or breed your own.

Mantis are superbly designed hunting and eating insects.

Most flying insects are good as food for mantis, except for biting and stinging insects. I frequently use dragonflies as they are common where I live but care is needed, as large dragonflies can inflict damage on small mantis.

Cockroaches are good as food because they are active and attract the attention of the mantis. Turkestan roaches are ideal as they are mobile but cannot climb plastic; Dubia roaches are good for the larger species but monitor them in the cage until they have been eaten, as they are strong insects and not all mantis can subdue them properly.

Superworms, *Zophobas morio*, are also a good backup if other food is not available. If there is no live food available a hungry mantis can sometimes be tempted to eat small amounts of fresh liver if it is held in tweezers and gently placed at its mouthparts.

Certain species of mantis, such as the Orchid mantis (*Hymenopus coronatus*), reportedly need a regular supply of flying insects rather than cockroaches or crickets to form proper oothecae.

Mantis like to drink water and they should be sprayed at least daily. Even those that come from dry climates need to drink but these species from drier environments need a cage that has sufficient ventilation so that the humidity does not stay elevated for long.

Temperature

Many species require temperatures between 20°C to 25°C (68°F - 77°F), so room temperature will normally be sufficient. Those from tropical areas will need higher temperatures, so you may need to provide heating. Reasonably high humidity is important for most species, especially when they are about to moult.

There are exceptions, of course, and *Gongylus gongylodes*, for example, needs high temperatures up to 35°C (95°F) and a dry atmosphere (except when moulting).

Breeding

One of the greatest challenges with mantis is getting them to mate successfully. Despite sensational stories to the contrary, it is not necessary for the female to eat the male but it does happen if certain precautions are not taken.

The females of most species will only be ready for mating about six weeks after the final skin change. Any attempts at breeding before she is ready will normally result in the loss of the male.

After six weeks the female should be plump. Before introducing a male, feed the female heavily until she refuses any more food.

Mantis mating - *Tenodera* species

Although it varies by species, mating often takes place in the afternoon.

I prefer to place the male on the lower part of a plant with open branches and not too many leaves. If the male is prone to fly, this can be put inside a large cage. Otherwise, the plant can be placed on a table in a room, with the doors and windows closed. I find that a fan blowing gently on the plant calms the male, as any movement he makes is masked by the breeze.

Mantis will eat most insects, including others of their own species - and even during mating, like this *Rhombodera* female.

The plant allows the male to clamber up to the female if he feels safe and, if the plant is not in a cage, it enables you to step in if the female looks like she is about to attack him. If things do go wrong, the male also has the ability to fly to freedom, which he will not have in a small cage.

Once the male is settled, introduce the female about 15cm (6") above him onto a stout branch, preferably facing away from him. If possible, try to entice her to eat a fly, cockroach or butterfly.

While the female is eating she may turn, so that she is facing down the branch. The male will then have to be carefully moved so he is above her.

If all goes well, he will slowly advance on the female, stopping frequently. He will then hop onto her back and copulation will take place. Be ready to intervene if the female is not receptive and be aware that the female can move very fast!

Mating normally lasts between thirty minutes and a couple of hours. The male may stay on the female's back after copulation simply because it is the safest place to be. It is best to remove him as soon as it is practical. However, if they have not separated by late evening, I put the plant with the mating pair inside a large flexarium and leave it overnight. I rarely lose males as the cage is sufficiently large that the male can escape the notice of the female if they part during the night.

A problem that often arises when trying to start a colony of mantis is the speed with which the males mature compared to the females. In many species the males will have matured and died before the females from the same batch are ready to mate. This is reportedly a way to avoid siblings mating but it can prove very troublesome if you only have a limited number of nymphs.

One way to overcome this is to keep males in a cooler room and restrict their food slightly, while keeping the females warmer and better fed. Orchid mantis are notorious for 'unsynchronised' maturing.

Egg laying and care of oothecae

The female will often lay her first ootheca the day after mating but this is not always the case and several days or even weeks may pass before she lays. She may also lay oothecae without mating but these will be infertile, except for a few exceptional species that are parthenogenic.

A female can lay from four to ten oothecae during her life. Although one mating will be enough for many of the oothecae to be produce

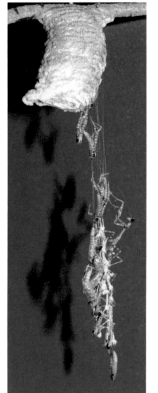

nymphs, it is better if she mates after every third or fourth ootheca to ensure optimum fertility of the eggs.

The ootheca should be left to harden before any attempt is made to remove it. If possible, leave it where it was laid to hatch undisturbed. If the ootheca is removed it should be glued or pinned with care at the top of a cage. The nymphs will hang down as they hatch, so it is important to leave space below the ootheca.

Oothecae should be sprayed every day or two. It should only be a light spray but drying out is a common reason for the non-hatching of nymphs from an ootheca. Over-spraying will also kill the eggs.

Deroplatys nymphs hatching from their ootheca.

Care of nymphs

When they have first hatched, most nymphs do not eat straight away and it may be several days before they will grab their first fruit fly. Water is important, so light spraying is necessary but be careful not to leave large droplets in the cage as the nymphs can drown easily.

Given how fast nymphs can run and how good fruit flies are at escaping, I put a couple of small tubs of mashed banana in a medium-sized wooden framed, net-sided cage, roughly 30cm by 30cm by 30cm high (12" x 12" x 12"). I then add a batch of mantis hatchlings and tip a complete culture of fruit flies in before closing the door quickly. The fruit flies will breed in the cage and, apart from daily spraying with water, the mantis hatchlings can be left undisturbed for a week or longer.

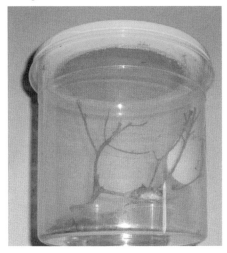

Simple cage for mantis nymphs

I also use cylindrical plastic tubs about 30cm (12") in diameter (as shown in the photograph) set up in a similar manner, with a circle of fine plastic mesh hot-glued onto a large hole cut into the lid. The downside of these plastic tubs is that access is via the lid. When it is opened, both mantis nymphs and fruit flies are quick in their attempts to escape.

If you are using mashed banana as food for fruit flies in a cage with nymphs, sprinkle some bran or oats on top of the banana, otherwise some of the nymphs may get stuck in the wet banana.

After the second moult, the nymphs should either be separated or split into smaller groups. Some individuals and some sexes (differing by species) will grow faster than others and keeping them together will encourage cannibalism.

Sexing nymphs

Sexual dimorphism shown by the Orchid mantis *Hymenopus coronatus* from Malaysia

By about the third instar the difference between the sexes may become apparent. Some species exhibit more extreme sexual dimorphism than others.

As they get older, even in species with less obvious differences, it might be possible to distinguish males from females by looking at their abdominal segments. When viewed from the underside, males have eight abdominal segments and females have six but it is not always obvious.

The differences are easier to determine in some species than others. Sexing mantis can be very difficult, especially when they are young.

Caution

Aside from the fascination that comes from rearing mantis, and the possibility of it becoming a time-consuming hobby, there are very few problems.

Some larger mantis can be aggressive and will make warning displays to an approaching predator, fully prepared to defend itself. With sharp claws and fast reflexes a large mantis could inflict serious damage on an unwary reptile. This is only likely to hap-

Mantis warning display

pen if the mantis is too large for the hungry reptile. I have fed several full-grown female *Cilnia* mantis – a species known to be aggressive - to adult Panther chameleons without problems.

The laws regarding the keeping of mantis vary by country, so you should check locally. In Europe it is illegal to keep *Mantis religiosa*, although at the time of writing all other non-protected species are permitted. In the US certain restrictions seem to apply to different species in different states.

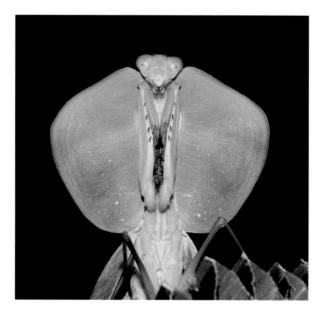

With so many beautiful and fascinating species available, such as this Shield Mantis, *Choeradodis rhombicollis*, from Ecuador, it is no surprise that keeping mantis has become a popular hobby – and a reason why people breed other insects as feeder food!

Phasmids

Introduction

The roughly 2,500 species of Phasmids are the ultimate camouflage experts of the insect world and include stick insects and leaf insects.

As herbivores, they are nutritious as long as they are not feeding on poisonous plants. As a feeder food they have one big advantage – when a colony is breeding well it can produce lots of individuals. A single female *Phoebaeticus serratipes* can lay hundreds of eggs.

Another advantage for some people is that as plant eaters, phasmids don't smell and generally need little maintenance.

Species

Goliath Stick Insect *Eurycnema goliath*

Stick insects vary in size from a few centimetres in length to some that grow to over half a metre long. Some are as thin as a piece of string, whereas female Malay Tree Nymphs (*Heteropteryx dilitata*) are among the heaviest insects on the planet – and armed with vicious spines on their head and legs.

The Indian Stick Insect (*Carausius morosus*) is a favourite in schools, being easy to breed. *Phoebaeticus* and *Pharnacia* are among the species that would also be safe as food due to the absence of spines but there are many others – too many to name here.

Fast hatching eggs, non-toxic food plant, lack of spines and easy to rear are the main criteria for choosing a species to breed as food.

Life Cycle

A stick insect hatches from an egg and goes through several skin changes until it reaches adulthood. In some species there is little difference between the younger stages and the adults. Many species exhibit strong sexual dimorphism even before becoming adult, with the male nymphs often being thinner and having more obvious wing buds.

The length of the life cycle varies greatly from a few months in some species to three years or so in the case of the Malay Tree Nymph.

Some eggs hatch quickly but other species can take up to 18 months, hardly worth the wait if you are going to use the nymphs as food. The fastest I have seen were *Marmessoidea rosea* eggs that hatched in under four weeks; that is exceptional.

A tall cage made from two laundry baskets

Housing

A large airy cage, sufficiently tall that the stick insect can hang down when changing skin, is needed. Branches of the food plant are put in plastic water bottles to keep the food fresh, so the cage will also need to be tall enough to accommodate the bottle and the branches. The mouth of the bottle should be plugged so that stick or leaf insects cannot walk down the stems and drown in the water. If you are fortunate enough to have a cage big enough to put a potted plant in, so much the better.

An inexpensive, easy-to-make Phasmid cage

Some keepers use substrate, such as peat or vermiculite, to keep the humidity high in the cage. I don't as this makes cleaning out the cage and finding the scattered eggs more difficult. Paper kitchen towel or even newspaper laid on the floor of the cage is sufficient and can be easily replaced when necessary.

Feeding

Each species has different requirements for food in the wild but in captivity many will accept bramble, rose and oak. Some will also eat privet, eucalyptus and even ivy. A few species are so specialised that they will refuse anything but one type of plant.

In northern Europe, bramble is used extensively as it is widely accepted by most common species and leaves can be found even in the hardest winters.

Newly hatched nymphs of some species can be problematic, as they will often not feed. Although surrounded by their food plant some will starve to death after wandering aimlessly for days. Leaf insects are notoriously difficult to get to eat their first meal.

If possible, try putting the newly hatched nymphs in with older ones; other nymphs eating nearby often stimulates youngsters. A light breeze can be effective, as this encourages the nymphs to move about more, and I have successfully used a small computer cooling fan placed next to the cage to create the slight air movement required. Clipping

Giant Leaf Insect *Phyllium giganteum* – too well camouflaged to be used as food.

the edges of leaves or ripping them can expose fresh edges which can also get the youngsters started.

When the nymphs are younger most need spraying with water every day. As they get older, the need for spraying reduces, subject to temperature. Most species benefit from a light spray every few days but check first as there are a few that dislike high humidity.

Temperature

Most stick insects will thrive at room temperatures, between 22°C and 27°C (72°F - 80°F). Indian stick insects will breed well at lower temperatures, for example 18°C (65°F).

Breeding

In many species, such as *Eurycnema goliath*, there is strong sexual dimorphism making it easy to tell the sexes apart. However, a male is not always necessary for the successful production of fertile eggs. Species such as the Australian Spiny Stick Insect (*Extatosoma tiaratum*) will lay hundreds of eggs without ever mating but if she does mate then the number of eggs often increases and the length of time before they hatch is reduced.

Mostly, mating is as simple as putting a male in with the female. With a few species e.g. Malay Tree Nymph and the Madagascan Blue (*Achrioptera fallax*), the male is so eager to mate that he will hinder the female from laying eggs and should be removed after a successful pairing. He should only being reintroduced every other week or so.

Achrioptera fallax shows marked sexual dimorphism.

Care of eggs

The eggs of most stick insects resemble some sort of plant seed. In some cases the eggs are just dropped by the female, to lay among the leaf litter until they hatch. Females of other species will push the eggs into the soil with strong ovipositors. A few glue their eggs along branches or under leaves.

The time taken for eggs to hatch varies a lot. Even within the same species, and often the same batch of eggs, there can be a period of several months between nymphs hatching. Some species will hatch in as little as two months but most take around four to six months, with a few species only hatching after more than a year.

A higher humidity, coupled with good ventilation, and an even temperature are the normal requirements for the eggs to hatch. If kept too dry the eggs will dry out; too wet and mould will form on them. This is not always fatal, so don't throw away eggs that have a little mould – try to wipe it off gently.

Room temperature is normally good enough for hatching eggs but anything between 20°C and 27°C (68°F - 80°F) should work well.

There are several types of containers and methodologies used to hatch eggs. Some are aimed at the specific requirements for rarer species, such as providing a humid atmosphere while avoiding contact with moisture, but the following system will work with most species that will be used as food:

Line a 5 litre plastic box with several layers of paper kitchen towel. Make of lot of holes, about 4 mm (0.15") diameter, in the lid of the box. Place the eggs on the paper towel and spray lightly once every few days. Most species will hatch well in such a set-up.

Caution

The disadvantages are that, by their very nature, Phasmids are hard to see and many predators will lose interest in them unless they are active. Another problem is that some are armed with nasty spines which may inflict injury to the mouth or even the body of the reptile.

Some New World species can spray a stinging liquid at its attacker.

I once had a surplus of male Australian Spiny Stick Insects which I fed to several adult Pan-

Female Malay Tree Nymph *Heteropteryx dilitata*. Note the spines. This species is quite aggressive and not suitable for use as food.

ther chameleons. This is a more active stick insect than most and the males often fly when disturbed, showing off their bright pink wings. All the Panther chameleons readily ate the stick insects but one developed a swollen tongue. Whether this was due to the spines on the insect or not is impossible to tell; none of the other chameleons showed any problems.

Stick insects can add variety to your animal's diet. Nymphs of species like *Phoebaeticus serratipes* from Malaysia lack spines and are easy to breed. But, like most phasmids, you will need patience while waiting the six months or so for the eggs to hatch.

Author

David Haggett's fascination with insects started many years ago as a child in England. Later, he was fortunate that his work gave him the opportunity to travel extensively, taking him to diverse and exotic locations. This enabled him, in his spare time, to pursue his interest in natural history, which includes not just entomology but also reptiles.

While living in South Africa, David started breeding chameleons and various insects. This soon developed into a full-time occupation, along with writing. Currently living in Malaysia, he is continuing his study of insects.

David's first book - Exotic Chameleons in South Africa, their Care and Breeding -quickly became popular among chameleon enthusiasts in that country. This is David's fifth book and he has contributed articles to magazines in South Africa and other countries.

Contact me at: *davidhaggett@mantispress.co.uk*

Acknowledgements

Over the several decades I have been interested in bugs and reptiles many, many people have helped me by providing guidance and even breeding stock. Some I have met personally and others have helped through forums and e-mail. To all of these: many thanks for your unselfish assistance.

My wife and daughter have been very supportive and have put up with some strange guests in our house, occasionally not in the cages provided. My daughter has asked, on more than one occasion, what it would be like to grow up in a normal household. Happily, she will never know!

As always, my wife has been generous in her suggestions and editing skills. Any errors are entirely mine and not hers.

Further Information

New photographs, additional tips and more information about this book and breeding insects for feeder food can be found on the related Facebook page:

> https://www.facebook.com/breeding.insects.as.feeder.food

If you are interested in exotic insects, you may enjoy browsing the Facebook page: https://www.facebook.com/fantastic.insects

Other books by the author

Beginner's Guide to keeping Exotic Chameleons

Exotic Chameleons in South Africa, their care and breeding

Visit www.mantispress.co.uk for details of these books and others.

Made in the USA
Middletown, DE
16 February 2020